SELF-PACED PHONICS
A Text for Education

Second Edition

G. Thomas Baer
Illinois State University

Merrill, an imprint of Prentice Hall
Upper Saddle River, New Jersey   Columbus, Ohio

Library of Congress Cataloging-in-Publication Data

Baer, G. Thomas
    Self-paced phonics : a text for education / G. Thomas Baer. — 2nd ed.
      p. cm.
    Includes bibliographical references.
    — ISBN 0-13-956889-1
    1. Reading—Phonetic method. 2. Reading (Elementary)   I. Title.
LB1573.3.B34 1999
372.46′5—dc21   97-45705
                                                      CIP

Cover photo: Colored Plastic Letters/H. Armstrong Roberts
Editor: Bradley J. Potthoff
Production Editor: Mary M. Irvin
Design Coordinator: Karrie M. Converse
Text Designer: Linda M. Robertson
Cover Designer: Ceri Fitzgerald
Production Manager: Pamela D. Bennett
Director of Marketing: Kevin Flanagan
Marketing Manager: Suzanne Stanton
Advertising/Marketing Coordinator: Julie Shough

This book was set in Zapf Calligraphic by Carlisle Communications, Inc., and was printed and bound by R.R. Donnelley & Sons Company. The cover was printed by Phoenix Color Corp.

 © 1999 by Prentice-Hall, Inc.
Simon & Schuster/A Viacom Company
Upper Saddle River, New Jersey 07458

Printed in the United States of America

10 9 8 7 6 5 4 3 2 1

ISBN: 0-13-956889-1

Prentice-Hall International (UK) Limited, *London*
Prentice-Hall of Australia Pty. Limited, *Sydney*
Prentice-Hall of Canada, Inc., *Toronto*
Prentice-Hall Hispanoamericana, S. A., *Mexico*
Prentice-Hall of India Private Limited, *New Delhi*
Prentice-Hall of Japan, Inc., *Tokyo*
Simon & Schuster Asia Pte. Ltd., *Singapore*
Editora Prentice-Hall do Brasil, Ltda., *Rio de Janeiro*

Preface

Although phonics has been with us in one form or another from colonial times to the present, it continues to head the list of reading topics that elicit the most emotional responses—not only from detractors within the teaching profession, but also from without. Based on the conclusions of reports such as *Becoming a Nation of Readers: The Report of the Commission of Reading* (1984) and *Beginning to Read: Thinking and Learning About Print* (1990), however, there is strong evidence to suggest that children who are taught phonics at the beginning stages of reading instruction do better than those who are not. Clearly, the question regarding phonics instruction no longer appears to be whether it should be included in beginning instruction; instead, the essential question is one of determining how phonics can be taught most effectively.

The purpose of this text is to provide prospective elementary teachers with instruction that will assist them in developing a sound understanding of both the content and pedagogy of phonics. This instruction is accomplished through the following text features:

1. Education majors will be able to complete the text with a minimal amount of direct instruction. With little formal instruction required, faculty who already face content overload will find the text teacher-friendly.

2. The text is designed to complement developmental reading methods textbooks that typically cover phonics in a superficial manner.

3. The text uses sound learning principles by providing students with meaningful practice and immediate feedback. The chapter practices, cumulative reviews, pretest, and post-test provide students with numerous opportunities to work with the content of phonics.

4. The text recognizes that, although phonics is only *one* of several word recognition techniques, it remains the one that is least understood by prospective teachers.

Input from students who have used the text over the past six years, along with evaluative feedback from reading professionals in the field, have been used to expand and strengthen the second edition of this text. Special attention has been paid to including more examples that illustrate particular phonics elements and to expanding significantly the practices and cumulative reviews so that they provide increased opportunities for students to work with both the content and pedagogy of phonics.

ACKNOWLEDGMENTS

Many thanks to the reviewers of this text for their insights and comments: Barbara Blair, State University College at Potsdam; Patricia Terrell Campbell, East Carolina University; Marie F. Doan, Florida Atlantic University; Shirley A. Reed, University of Montevallo, Emeritus; and Rochelle Wardell, Illinois State University.

Contents

1

■ ■ ■ ■ ■

Introduction

The question about the value of phonics instruction has long been controversial. Emans (1968) points out that the emphasis on phonics instruction has changed several times over the past two centuries. Instruction has shifted from one extreme—no phonics instruction—to the other extreme—phonics instruction as the major method of word-recognition instruction—and back again. Emans (1968) also points out that "each time that phonics has been returned to the classroom, it usually has been revised into something quite different from what it was when it was discarded" (p. 607). Currently, most beginning reading programs include a significant component of phonics instruction.

Phonics, however, is not the cure-all for reading ills that some believe it to be. Rudolph Flesch's book, *Why Johnny Can't Read* (1955), although it did bring the phonics debate to the attention of the public, typifies the kind of literature that takes a naive approach to a very complex problem. As Heilman (1981) points out, "Flesch's suggestions for teaching were quite primitive, consisting primarily of lists of words each presenting different letter-sound patterns. Thus, Flesch did not actually provide teaching materials that schools and teachers could use" (p. 3). Still, this kind of approach, which reduced learning to read to the simple task of memorizing the alphabet and learning its letter-to-sound correspondences through an emphasis on writing, attracted disciples who vigorously carried forth its message.

Teachers must remember that phonics is but one of the major word recognition methods that also include whole-word methodology, contextual analysis, structural analysis, and dictionary use. These methods do not conflict with one another. If one is a proponent of phonics instruction, one does not have to be opposed to learning words via the other word-recognition methods. Rather, it should be the goal of reading teachers to develop children's skills in all these methods for three basic reasons:

1. Children will find some methods more suited to their abilities than others. Research has consistently shown that no one method is best for

teaching all children. Thus, each child should be given opportunities to learn and use all word-recognition methods.

2. Some words are learned more easily by using one method over another. For example, it may be more effective to teach an irregularly spelled word through a whole-word emphasis rather than a phonics emphasis.

3. When children encounter unknown words, they often use the various word-recognition techniques in concert, not as isolated skills having no relationship to one another.

Over the past 30 years, several studies and reports on reading stand out as having made major impacts on present-day phonics instruction. The first-grade reading studies (Bond & Dykstra, 1967) completed during the 1964–1965 school year provided data that have had an important and lasting influence on today's reading materials. Although the data seemed to indicate that no one method of teaching reading was superior to all others, they did suggest that an earlier and increased emphasis on phonics instruction would strengthen basal reading programs.

After an extensive critical analysis of research that examined the various approaches to beginning reading, Chall (1967) came to the following conclusions:

> My review of the research from the laboratory, the classroom, and the clinic points to the need for a correction in beginning reading instructional methods. Most schoolchildren in the United States are taught to read by what I have termed a meaning emphasis method. Yet, the research from 1912 to 1965 indicates that a code-emphasis method—i.e., one that views beginning reading as essentially different from mature reading and emphasizes learning of the printed code for the spoken language— produces better results, at least up to the point where sufficient evidence seems to be available, the end of the third grade.
>
> The results are better, not only in terms of the mechanical aspects of literacy alone, as was once supposed, but also in terms of the ultimate goals of reading instruction—comprehension and possibly even speed of reading. The long-existing fear that an initial code emphasis produces readers who do not read for meaning or with enjoyment is unfounded. On the contrary, the evidence indicates that better results in terms of reading for meaning are achieved with the programs that emphasize code at the start than with the programs that stress meaning at the beginning (p. 307).

The National Academy of Education's Commission on Education and Public Policy, with the sponsorship of the National Institute of Education, established the Commission on Reading in 1983 to "locate topics on which there has been appreciable research and scholarship . . . and gather panels of experts from within the Academy and elsewhere to survey, interpret and synthesize research findings" (Anderson, Hiebert, Scott, & Wilkinson, 1984, p. viii). The Commission on Reading's efforts resulted in the influential report *Becoming a Nation of Readers*. In the forward to this report, Robert Glaser, president of the National Academy of Education, writes,

> The last two decades of research and scholarship on reading, building on the past, have produced an array of information which is unparalleled in its understanding of the underlying processes in the comprehension of language. Although reading abilities and disabilities require further investigation, present knowledge, combined with the centrality of literacy in the educational process, make the report cause for optimism. Gains from reading research demonstrate the power of new spectra of research findings and methodologies to account for the cognitive activities entailed in school learning. And because, in the schools and classrooms across the country, reading is an essential tool for success, we can hope for significant advances in academic achievement as the policies and practices outlined in these pages become more widespread (Anderson et al., 1984, p. viii).

The Commission on Reading concluded that phonics instruction should hold an important place in beginning reading instruction and recommended that "teachers of beginning reading should present well-designed phonics instruction" (Anderson et al., 1984, p. 118).

More recently, in work supported by the U.S. Department of Education Cooperative Agreement with the Reading Research and Education Center of the University of Illinois at Urbana-Champaign, Marilyn J. Adams's work, *Beginning to Read: Thinking and Learning About Print*, has extended our understanding and knowledge on the issue of phonics and its role in learning to read. After an exhaustive review of pertinent basic and applied research, Adams (1990) concludes:

> In summary, deep and thorough knowledge of letters, spelling patterns, and words, and of the phonological translations of all three, are of inescapable importance to both skillful reading and its acquisition. By extension, instruction designed to develop children's sensitivity to spellings and their relations to pronunciations should be of paramount importance in the development of reading skills. This is, of course, precisely what is intended of good phonic instruction (p. 416).

Hence, the question regarding phonics instruction no longer appears to be whether or not it should be included in beginning instruction. Instead, the essential question is one of determining how phonics can be taught most effectively. To assist teachers in teaching phonics effectively, several basic principles should underlie their actions:

1. Phonics must be viewed as a means to an end, not an end in itself. The purpose of phonics is to assist children in systematically decoding words that are unknown to them by teaching them the relationships that exist between letters and speech sounds.

2. Phonics will not work for all children. As with other methods of teaching reading, its effectiveness will run the gamut from ineffective to extremely effective. A challenge for teachers is to determine the proper match between phonics and the individual child.

3. Phonics helps only if the unknown word is part of the reader's speaking-listening vocabulary. Take, for instance, the sentence, "The boy ran to the sliet." Although you can venture a guess about the proper pronunciation of *sliet*, you have no way of knowing whether you are correct because it is a nonsense word and not part of your speaking-listening vocabulary.

4. Phonics is a skill that must be used in conjunction with the skills of contextual and structural analysis. Smith (1982) identifies the relationship between phonics and context: "Phonic strategies cannot be expected to eliminate all the uncertainty when the reader has no idea what the word might be. But if the reader can reduce alternatives in advance—by making use of non-visual information related both to reading and to the subject matter of the text—then phonics can be made most efficient. One way to reduce uncertainty in advance is to employ the mediating technique of making use of context" (p. 147).

5. In learning phonics, children must have the opportunity to see, hear, and say the components they are asked to learn. Initial instruction and practice in phonics should, therefore, concentrate on oral activities. To accomplish this goal, teachers need to model continually the correct sounds of letters and words, and children need numerous opportunities to say these sounds and words. It should be kept in mind that too many teaching materials require students to learn and/or practice phonics in a silent—and therefore ineffective—manner, through the use of workbooks and other paper-and-pencil activities.

6. Phonics can best be taught by using both synthetic (explicit) and analytic (implicit) approaches to instruction. Although it must be understood that there is more than one significant difference between the synthetic and analytic approaches to phonics, the most basic difference between the two should be noted. Synthetic programs generally emphasize the learning of individual sounds, often in isolation, and follow with instruction that teaches children how to blend these individual sounds to form words (a part-to-whole approach). For instances, in the word *bat*, children would first sound out the isolated sounds (/b/ buh, /ă/ ah, /t/ tuh) and then blend them together to pronounce *bat*. Analytic programs, on the other hand, begin with whole words and identify individual sounds as part of those words. Efforts are made to avoid pronouncing letter sounds in isolation (a whole-to-part approach). On this point, the Commission on Reading (Anderson et al., 1984) writes: "In the judgment of the Commission, isolating the sounds

associated with most letters and teaching children to blend the sounds of letters together to try to identify words are useful instructional strategies. These are the strategies of explicit phonics. However, research provides insufficient justification for strict adherence to either overall philosophy. Probably, the best strategy would draw from both approaches" (p. 42).

In *Beginning to Read: Thinking and Learning About Print—A Summary,* Stahl, Osborn, & Lehr (1990) recommend the use of explicit instruction in phonics:

> Because most phonemes cannot be pronounced without a vowel, many programs avoid or limit the use of isolated phonemes in their instruction. This practice often leads to potentially confusing instruction. The advantages of asking students to articulate phonemes in isolation outweigh the disadvantages.
>
> Because children have special difficulty analyzing the phonemic structure of words, reading programs should include explicit instruction in blending (p. 126).

7. "Phonics instruction should be kept simple and it should be completed by the end of second grade for most children" (Anderson et al., 1984, p. 118).

Through improved instruction, gains in reading achievement will be realized. Yet it has become painfully clear that too many teachers received inadequate emphasis on phonics in preservice coursework and lack basic knowledge that would allow them to present well-conceived and effective phonics instruction.

The following chapters are designed to overcome this limiting factor by providing prospective teachers with a phonics knowledge base and teaching strategies. Both will enable them to provide beginning readers with programs based on sound principles.

■ ■ ■   CHAPTER 1: PRACTICE

1. Phonics (is, is not) the single most important factor in reading success. (Circle one.)

2. For most children, phonics instruction should be completed by the end of _____ grade.

3. Phonics is most effective when it is utilized with skills such as

   _____ _____ and _____

   _____ .

4. The purpose of phonics is to assist children in systematically decoding words that are unknown to them by teaching them the relationships that exist between _____ and _____ .

5. Phonics programs that emphasize the learning of individual sounds, often in isolation, and follow with instruction that teaches children how to blend these individual sounds to form words are known as explicit, or _____ , programs.

6. Think back to your earliest school experiences. Visualize the methods by which you were taught to read. What role did phonics play?

_____

_____

_____

_____

_____

_____

_____

_____

_____

_____

7. Why is it instructionally ineffective to have children practice phonics by filling out workbook pages and ditto sheets?

_____

_____

_____

_____

_____

_____

_____

_____

8. Explain the following statement: "Phonics must be viewed as a means to an end, not an end in itself."

_____

_____

_____

_____

_____

2

■ ■ ■ ■ ■

Phonics Pretest

This pretest is designed to provide readers with feedback that should assist them in assessing their knowledge of phonics content. An analysis of results will help identify specific content problems and provide a focus as readers work through the text.

MATCHING

Match the words listed below with the appropriate definitions numbered 1 to 10.

a. phoneme   f. grapheme
b. digraph   g. macron
c. syllable   h. closed syllable
d. phonogram   i. consonant blend
e. phonics   j. diphthong

_____ 1. Two letters that stand for a single phoneme.

_____ 2. A letter or combination of letters that represents a phoneme.

_____ 3. Any syllable that ends with a consonant phoneme.

_____ 4. A method in which basic phonetics, the study of human speech sounds, is used to teach beginning reading.

_____ 5. The smallest *sound* unit of a language that distinguishes one word from another.

_____ 6. A letter sequence comprised of a vowel grapheme and an ending consonant grapheme(s).

_____ 7. A *single vowel sound* made up of a blend of two vowel sounds in immediate sequence and pronounced in one syllable.

_____ 8. Sounds in a syllable represented by two or more letters that are blended together without losing their own identities.

_____ 9. A unit of pronunciation that consists of a vowel alone or a vowel with one or more consonants.

_____ 10. The symbol placed over a vowel letter to show it is pronounced as a long sound.

TRUE-FALSE

_____ 11. The irregularity of vowel sounds is a basic problem of phonics.

_____ 12. The *schwa* sound is generally spelled in a consistent manner.

_____ 13. Phonics is the most important skill required for effective reading.

_____ 14. Almost any letter may, at some time, be silent.

_____ 15. A grapheme may be composed of one or more letters.

_____ 16. Each syllable must contain only one vowel letter.

_____ 17. In decoding multisyllabic words, syllabication should precede the application of vowel generalizations.

_____ 18. There are approximately 100 ways to spell the 44 phonemes.

_____ 19. By the time the average child enters school, his or her auditory discrimination skills are fully developed.

_____ 20. The history of phonics shows that a phonics approach to teaching reading has been looked upon favorably by most reading authorities over the past 50 years.

MULTIPLE CHOICE

_____ 21. Which of the following is a sound?
   a. grapheme
   b. vowel
   c. digraph
   d. none of the above

_____ 22. Which of the following words contains an open syllable?
   a. love
   b. son
   c. through
   d. fire

_____ 23. Which of the following words contains a digraph?
   a. fly
   b. bring
   c. blond
   d. home

_____ 24. Which of the following words contains letters that represent a diphthong?
   a. low
   b. meat
   c. through
   d. boy

_____ 25. How many phonemes are represented by the word *night*?
   a. 1
   b. 2
   c. 3
   d. 5

_____ 26. How many phonemes are represented by the word *boat*?
   a. 1
   b. 2
   c. 3
   d. 4

_____ 27. Which of the following pairs contains the same vowel phoneme?
   a. book—room
   b. too—shoe
   c. wool—food
   d. none of the above

_____ 28. Which of the following letters do not represent phonemes that are identified by their own name?
   a. t and s
   b. b and d
   c. y and z
   d. c and q

_____ 29. Which of the following consonant letters are most phonemically inconsistent in representing more than one sound?
   a. b and d
   b. c and s
   c. r and t
   d. m and p

_____ 30. Which of the following letter pairs represents a consonant blend?
   a. ch
   b. br
   c. th
   d. -ng

_____ 31. Which of the following nonsense words would most likely represent the "soft c" sound?
  a. cint
  b. cule
  c. coble
  d. calope

_____ 32. Which of the following nonsense words would most likely represent the "hard g" sound?
  a. giltion
  b. seg
  c. buge
  d. gymp

_____ 33. Which of the following consonant letters affects the vowel that precedes it?
  a. m
  b. t
  c. r
  d. none of the above

_____ 34. Which of the following words does not contain a consonant blend?
  a. fruit
  b. why
  c. blue
  d. flower

_____ 35. Which of the following words contains a closed syllable?
  a. low
  b. doubt
  c. dough
  d. boy

Circle the item in each list below that does not belong. Explain your reason for each choice.

36. sl   tr   bl   th   cl

_____

_____

_____

37. sh   wh   st   ng   ch

_____

_____

_____

38. a y i s w

_____

_____

_____

39. owl out low pound

_____

_____

_____

40. gym gum game go

_____

_____

_____

The following questions should be answered by using the vowel generalizations that are often taught in elementary schools. Each question
requires the vowel pronunciation contained in a nonsense word.

_____ 41. The *a* in *kaic* has the same sound as that found in:
   a. art
   b. may
   c. map
   d. none of the above

_____ 42. The *e* in *clek* has the same sound as that found in:
   a. be
   b. err
   c. end
   d. none of the above

_____ 43. The *o* in *kote* has the same sound as that found in:
   a. not
   b. or
   c. go
   d. boy

_____ 44. The *a* in *psa* has the same sound as that found in:
   a. art
   b. may
   c. map
   d. none of the above

_____ 45. The *i* in *sirp* has the same sound as that found in:
   a. in
   b. girl
   c. high
   d. none of the above

_____ 46. The *a* in *woab* has the same sound as that found in:
    a. art
    b. may
    c. map
    d. none of the above

_____ 47. The *u* in *kupp* has the same sound as that found in:
    a. hurt
    b. up
    c. rude
    d. none of the above

_____ 48. The *u* in *nue* has the same sound as that found in:
    a. hurt
    b. up
    c. use
    d. none of the above

Indicate where the syllabic divisions occur in the following vowel-consonant patterns, nonsense words, or real words. Knowledge of syllabication generalizations is essential. There are no consonant digraphs in questions 49 through 52 (C = consonant sound, V = vowel sound).

_____ 49. CVCVCC
    a. CVC-VCC
    b. CV-CVCC
    c. CVCV-CC
    d. CV-CV-CC

_____ 50. CVCCVC
    a. CV-CCVC
    b. CVCC-VC
    c. CVC-CVC
    d. CV-CC-VC

_____ 51. CVCCV
    a. CVC-CV
    b. CV-CCV
    c. CVCC-V
    d. C-V-CCV

_____ 52. CCVCVCC
    a. CCVC-VCC
    b. CCV-C-VCC
    c. CC-VC-VCC
    d. CCV-CVCC

_____ 53. intayed
   a. in-tay-ed
   b. in-tayed
   c. in-ta-yed
   d. intay-ed

_____ 54. makution
   a. ma-ku-tion
   b. mak-u-tion
   c. mak-u-ti-on
   d. ma-ku-ti-on

_____ 55. sleble
   a. sleb-le
   b. sleble
   c. sl-e-ble
   d. sle-ble

_____ 56. exanthema
   a. exan-the-ma
   b. ex-an-the-ma
   c. ex-an-them-a
   d. e-xan-the-ma

_____ 57. getker
   a. ge-tker
   b. get-ker
   c. getk-er
   d. getker

When a child meets an unknown word of more than one syllable, she or he must first be able to apply syllabication generalizations; second, she or he must be able to apply phonic generalizations. Using these generalizations, indicate how the following nonsense words would be pronounced correctly. (Although these words contain schwas, only long and short vowels will be used at this point.)

_____ 58. besatt
   a. bĕs-ătt
   b. bē-sătt
   c. bē-sātt
   d. bĕs-ātt

_____ 59. seklep
   a. sēk-lĕp
   b. sē-klĕp
   c. sĕk-lĕp
   d. sē-klēp

_____ 60. abstakatt
    a. ăb-stă-kătt
    b. ăb-stăk-ātt
    c. ăbs-tāk-ătt
    d. ăb-stā-kătt

■ ■ ■   **CHAPTER 2: PRACTICE**

Check your answers against those listed on pages 101–102. If you had difficulty, don't be discouraged. Rather, analyze your results to identify areas that gave you the most trouble. List these problem areas below. As you work through the text, use this information to provide a focus for your study.

_____

_____
_____
_____
_____
_____
_____
_____
_____
_____
_____
_____
_____
_____

■ ■ ■   **CUMULATIVE REVIEW OF CHAPTERS 1 AND 2**

1. The major word-recognition methods include phonics, whole-word methodology, _____ _____ , _____ _____ , and dictionary use.

2. Generally, the phonics instruction that appeared 35 years ago (is, is not) the same as that taught today. (Circle one.)

3. There (are, are not) significant research data that show the importance of phonics in beginning reading instruction. (Circle one.)

4. Why do most authorities suggest that phonics instruction should be completed by the end of second grade for most children?

_____

_____

_____

_____

_____

_____

_____

_____

_____

_____

5. Explain the difference between explicit phonics instruction and implicit phonics instruction.

_____

_____

_____

_____

_____

_____

_____

_____

6. From what you know about the whole language philosophy, do you believe it is compatible with the teaching of phonics? Explain.

_____

_____

_____

_____

_____

_____
_____
_____

7. If an unknown word is not part of a reader's speaking-listening vocabulary, why will phonics be of little value in the process of decoding?

_____
_____
_____
_____
_____
_____
_____
_____
_____

3

■ ■ ■ ■ ■

Phonics Vocabulary

Although a more detailed glossary appears at the end of this text (see the Glossary on page 116), an introduction to pertinent vocabulary at this juncture will assist readers as they read the text. Ultimately, the following vocabulary words should be learned to the point where all meanings are understood instantly (a state known as automaticity).

breve: The orthographic symbol (�’) placed over a vowel letter to show it is pronounced as a short sound (sometimes called an unglided vowel).

circumflex: The orthographic symbol (ˆ) placed above vowel graphemes to indicate pronunciation.

closed syllable: Any syllable that ends with a consonant phoneme (sound). Examples: come /m/; paste /t/; love /v/; ran /n/.

consonant: A sound represented by any letter of the English alphabet except *a, e, i, o, u.* Consonants are sounds made by closing or restricting the breath channel.

consonant blend: Sounds in a syllable represented by two or more letters that are blended together without losing their own identities. Examples: blue /b/ /l/; gray /g/ /r/; brown /b/ /r/; twig /t/ /w/; street /s/ /t/ /r/; flip /f/ /l/.

digraph: Two letters that stand for a single phoneme (sound). Examples: thin /th/; each /ē/; shop /sh/; boy /oi/; look /o͝o/; rang /ng/; few /o͞o/. (A digraph is simply a grapheme of two letters.)

diphthong: A single vowel sound made up of a glide from one vowel sound to another in immediate sequence and pronounced in one syllable. Examples: /oi/ in *oil* and *boy;* /ou/ in *house* and *owl.* (Phonetics would consider that some single-letter vowels represent diphthongs. For the purposes of teaching reading, however, only /oi/ and /ou/ will be considered diphthongs.)

grapheme: A letter or combination of letters that represents a phoneme (sound). Examples: the phoneme /b/ in *bat* is represented by the grapheme *b*; the phoneme /f/ in *phone* is represented by the grapheme *ph*. (There are over 200 different ways to spell the phonemes. For example, /f/ can take the form of *f* in *fine*, *gh* in *cough*, and *ph* in *elephant*. This is an example of three different graphemes representing the same phoneme.)

macron: The orthographic symbol (-) placed over a vowel letter to show it is pronounced as a long sound (sometimes called a glided vowel).

onset: The consonant sound(s) of a syllable that comes before the vowel sound. (Examples are included with the definition of *rime* below.)

open syllable: Any syllable that ends with a vowel sound (phoneme). Examples: see /ē/; may /ā/; boy /oi/; auto /ō/.

phoneme: The smallest *sound* unit of a language that distinguishes one word from another. Examples: the phoneme /h/ distinguishes *hat* from *at*; the words *tell* and *yell* are distinguished by their initial phonemes /t/ and /y/. (This text indicates that there are 44 phonemes in the American-English language. This number varies, however, according to different authorities and/or dialects. Slash marks, / /, will be used throughout the text to indicate that the reference is to a *sound* and not a *letter*.)

phonics: A method in which basic phonetics, the study of human speech sounds, is used to teach beginning reading. Teachers teach phonics, not phonetics.

phonogram: A letter sequence comprised of a vowel grapheme and an ending consonant grapheme(s), such as *-ig* in *wig, dig, big*, or the *-ack* in *back, tack, sack*. From phonograms we can generate word families.

r-controlled vowel: When a vowel letter is followed by the letter *r*, it affects the vowel sound so that it is neither short nor long. For example, in *her*, the vowel sound becomes /û/; in *dare*, it becomes /â/.

rime: The part of a syllable that includes the vowel sound and any consonant sound(s) that comes after it. The graphic representation of a rime is referred to as a *phonogram*. Following are examples of both onsets and rimes.

Word	*Onset*	*Rime*	*Phonogram*
mat	/m/	/at/	at
pig	/p/	/ig/	ig
at	—	/at/	at
split	/spl/	/it/	it

schwa sound: An unstressed sound commonly occurring in unstressed syllables. It is represented by the symbol /ə/ and closely resembles the short sound for *u*. Examples: *a* in *about*; *o* in *occur*; *i* in *pencil*; *u* in *circus*.

syllable: A unit of pronunciation consisting of a vowel alone or a vowel with one or more consonants. There can be only one vowel phoneme (sound) in each syllable.

umlaut: The orthographic symbol (¨) placed above vowel graphemes to indicate pronunciation.

vowel: A sound represented by *a, e, i, o, u,* and sometimes *y* and *w,* in the English alphabet. Vowels are sounds made without closing or restricting the breath channel.

■ ■ ■   CHAPTER 3: PRACTICE

1. Circle each of the following terms that refers to a sound.
   phoneme   vowel   grapheme   rime
   diphthong   digraph   consonant   phonogram

2. Vowel sounds are usually represented by the following letters:
   _____ , _____ , _____ , _____ , and _____ . Also, _____ and _____ sometimes represent vowels.

3. Circle each of the following words that contains an open syllable.
   son   go   dew
   love   through   fire

4. A _____ is composed of two letters that stand for a single phoneme.

5. Underline any consonant digraph contained in the following words.
   blue   bring   the   street   shut   chill   train

6. Underline any vowel digraph contained in the following words.
   dew   look   love   soup   boy   go   beat

7. A _____ is a special *single* vowel sound made up of a glide from one vowel to another. The phonemes that represent these sounds are /oi/ and /____/.

8. Each   syllable   must   contain   one   and   only   one   vowel _____ .

9. The orthographic symbol used to represent a long vowel sound is called a _____ .

10. The orthographic symbol used to represent a short vowel sound is called a _____ .

11. The letters that represent a diphthong are called a
_____ .

12. A(n) _____ syllable ends with a consonant phoneme.

13. A special kind of grapheme that consists of two letters is called a
_____ .

14. The study of human speech sounds is known as
_____ .

15. Define the following phonics terms. If you are able to define them in
your own words, you are well on your way to internalizing them and
achieving automaticity.

Vowel: _____

_____

_____

Grapheme: _____

_____

_____

Phoneme: _____

_____

_____

Consonant: _____

_____

_____

Syllable: _____

_____

_____

Macron: _____

_____

_____

Open syllable: _____

_____

_____

Breve: _____

_____

_____

Digraph: _____

_____

_____

Rime: _____

_____

_____

■ ■ ■ **CUMULATIVE REVIEW OF CHAPTERS 1 THROUGH 3**

1. What is the relationship between phonics and a person's speaking-listening vocabulary?

_____

_____

_____

_____

_____

_____

2. A (phonics, whole-word) emphasis would most likely be more effective with a word such as *pneumonia*. (Circle one.) Why?

_____

_____

_____

_____

_____

_____

3. The authors of *Becoming a Nation of Readers* (believe, do not believe) that the formal instruction of phonics should be extended into the intermediate grades. (Circle one.) Why?

_____

_____

_____

_____

_____

_____

4. (Synthetic, Analytic) programs generally emphasize the learning of individual sounds, often in isolation, and follow with instruction that teaches children how to blend these individual sounds to form words. (Circle one.) (Synthetic, Analytic) programs begin with whole words and identify individual sounds as part of those words. Efforts are made to avoid pronouncing letter sounds in isolation. (Circle one.) Can both of these approaches be taught to children without confusing them, or should teachers use only one or the other? Explain.

_____

_____

_____

_____

_____

_____

_____

5. Describe a situation where phonics and context would work hand in hand to help decode an unknown word.

_____

_____

_____

_____

6. I (did, did not) do well on the phonics pretest. (Circle one.) I suspect this was the case because:

_____

_____

_____

_____

_____

_____

_____

7. What are the differences between a digraph and diphthong?

_____

_____

_____

_____

_____

_____

_____

8. Underline any letters in the following words that represent a consonant blend.

   that   she   blend   church   street   why   sing

9. Identify a word in which the letter *w* functions as a vowel.

   _____

10. What is the difference between a consonant digraph and a consonant blend?

    _____

    _____

    _____

    _____

    _____

    _____

    _____

4

■ ■ ■ ■ ■

Readiness and Phonics

Ausubel (1959) defines readiness as "the adequacy of existing capacity in relation to the demands of a given learning task" (p. 246). This definition suggests that educators must not only examine learners and their capacities to learn, but that these capacities must be examined in light of the instructional methods to be used. Readiness is not something that exists in an absolute sense. It is quite possible that a child will be ready to learn under one set of instructional conditions and not be ready to learn under another.

The authors of *Becoming a Nation of Readers* (Anderson, Hiebert, Scott, & Wilkinson, 1984) recommend that "preschool and kindergarten reading readiness programs should focus on reading, writing, and oral language. Knowledge of letters and their sounds, words, stories, and question asking and answering are related to learning to read, but there is little evidence that such activities as coloring, cutting with a scissors, or discriminating shapes (except the shapes of letters) promote reading development" (pp. 117–118).

However, many more factors than those listed have been identified as having some influence on success in beginning reading. Intelligence, general health, vision, hearing, motor coordination, sex, listening ability, language development, auditory discrimination, visual discrimination, background experience, emotional adjustment, story sense, age, phonemic awareness, and knowledge of letter names head the list of factors that have been discussed in methods texts over the past 35 years (Harris & Smith, 1986; Searfoss & Readence, 1994; Spache & Spache, 1986). For the purposes of this text, only those factors relating most directly to a phonics approach to reading will be discussed at length.

VISION

Reading is a visual act that requires effective near-point (close) vision. Yet the types of tests often administered to children at the beginning stages of schooling simply measure far-point (distant) vision. Therefore, a cumulative

25

file that contains information indicating a child has successfully passed a vision test may be misleading. For this reason, teachers must be sensitive to signs in students that may indicate visual problems. Harris and Smith (1986) suggest that the following behaviors may be signs of visual problems:

1. Cocking the head to read with only one eye.
2. Holding the side of one's head when looking at the book or board.
3. Rubbing the eyes during reading.
4. Red eyes, watery eyes.
5. Holding the book too close to the face.
6. Holding the book at arm's length.
7. Complaints of headaches.
8. Squinting or other indications of strain.
9. Complaints of haziness or fading of printed symbols (p. 122).

HEARING

Auditory acuity, the ability to hear sounds of varying pitch and loudness, is an important factor in beginning reading. For instance, students who suffer hearing losses that affect their ability to hear high-frequency sounds may have difficulty in hearing certain consonants and consonant blends. Bond, Tinker, Wasson, & Wasson (1989) suggest that the following behaviors may be signs of auditory acuity problems:

1. Inattention during listening activities.
2. Frequent misunderstanding of oral directions or numerous requests for repetition of statements.
3. Turning one ear toward the speaker or thrusting head forward when listening.
4. Intent gaze at the speaker's face or strained posture while listening.
5. Monotone speech, poor pronunciation, or indistinct articulation.
6. Complaints of earache or hearing difficulty.
7. Insistence on closeness to sound sources.
8. Frequent colds, discharging ears, or difficult breathing (pp. 53–54).

If some of the above behaviors are observed in students, they should serve as an alert that there may be a physical problem with either sight or vision that is hindering effective learning. If these behaviors continue after closer scrutiny, a referral should be made to an appropriate school official who has been trained to deal with these problems.

ORAL LANGUAGE

Research has shown that a positive relationship exists between oral language and reading achievement (Blackman, 1984; Edmiaston, 1984; Rosenthal, Baker, & Ginsburg, 1983). It appears that oral language serves as an essential foundation on which reading instruction can and should be built. Furthermore, the Russian psychologist Vygotsky (Flavell, 1977) believed that, for young children to have a thought, they must say it out loud. In essence, if Vygotsky was correct, to silence young children is to silence their thoughts. For this reason, teachers must understand the significance of oral language in beginning reading instruction and learning in general, and to include activities in the curriculum that build on the language skills children bring to school.

Searfoss and Readence (1994) believe the rationale for oral language instruction should be based on three key processes:

1. Oral-language programs should utilize real experiences children have both in and out of school.

2. Oral-language development should be viewed as an integral part of the whole school day, planned but arising from naturally occurring events in the classroom.

3. Oral-language (speaking and listening) activities should lead naturally into using the tools of reading and writing. Activities designed to develop oral language should be integrated with reading and writing (p. 63).

The following is a sampling of the kinds of classroom activities that can be used to accomplish effective oral language instruction.

Activity 1: Read to children often. This activity has a positive effect on language development and can have an impact on children's attitudes toward reading. Jim Trelease's (1995) book, *The New-Read Aloud Handbook,* is an excellent source for the identification of books to be read aloud.

Activity 2: Provide children each day with numerous opportunities to express themselves. To accomplish this, set up situations that allow students to share experiences, ask questions, develop stories to be shared with others, resolve problems through language, and express attitudes and feelings. When teachers spend time at the beginning of the school day in activities such as "show and tell" or "bring and brag," they provide children with appropriate opportunities to express themselves orally.

Activity 3: Use patterned books along with rhymes, poems, and songs to help develop children's oral language. Because these types of materials are very predictable, children can join quickly in the reading process.

Activity 4:   Develop language experience stories using the children's natural language. In this process, children use language to explore a common experience. Once this oral exploration is exhausted, the teacher tells the class that she would like to write a story about their experiences. Using the children's own language, the teacher takes dictation and writes out their story, which is then used as reading material that children can begin to read. This procedure helps children come to understand that what can be said can be written down and preserved, to be used later through the act of reading.

PHONEMIC AWARENESS

The high correlation that exists between the ability to recognize spoken words as a sequence of individual sounds and reading achievement has been well established over the past 30 years (Bradley & Bryant, 1983; Calfee, Lindamood, & Lindamood, 1973; Ehri, 1979; Golinkoff, 1978; Tunmer & Nesdale, 1985). This correlation has generated interest in and research into the feasibility of teaching phonemic awareness to children at the kindergarten and first-grade levels. Lewkowicz (1980), in her analysis of ten tasks that have been used by researchers or classroom teachers to test or teach phonemic awareness, came to the conclusions that two of these tasks, segmentation and blending, were basic and belonged in beginning instructional programs. Examples of activities appropriate at the readiness level (defined as kindergarten to first grade) follow.

Activity 1:   Teach children to recognize auditorily and say the individual speech sounds. To accomplish this and other tasks in phonics, some authorities advocate an explicit (synthetic) approach, while others are proponents of an implicit (analytic) approach. It is the recommendation of this text that a combination of the two approaches will prove to be most effective (see the discussion beginning on pages 4–5). To illustrate the difference between the two approaches, /b/ could be taught in isolation by having children repeat or imitate the sound after it has been voiced by the teacher (explicit). In contrast, /b/ can also be taught by referring children to the first sound that they hear in a word such as *ball* without ever pronouncing the letter in isolation (implicit).

Even though research (Adams, 1990; Chall, 1983; Pflaum, Walberg, Karegianes, & Rasher, 1980) seems to favor the results of synthetic approaches, an overwhelming majority of basal texts take a strong analytic approach to teaching phonics, in part, because of two major criticisms of synthetic phonics. The first has to do with the belief held by some that a synthetic approach to reading will severely interfere with a child's ability to come to see reading as a meaningful process. The other relates to the fact that the isolation of some letter sounds produces "intrusive vowels" that distort the sounds as heard when pronouncing words. For instance, *cat* would be pronounced "cuh-a-tuh." The "uh" sounds following *c* and *t* are intrusive vowel sounds. Obviously, one cannot blend these sounds directly and come up with *cat*; some modification needs to be made during the blending process.

In keeping with the combined-approach recommendation of this text, more effort needs to be devoted to tasks that emphasize synthetic phonics. If teachers desire to accomplish a balance between analytic and synthetic phonics, they must develop many of their own materials.

Activity 2: Teach children to isolate initial sounds in words, which can be accomplished in several ways:

1. Teach children to hear and recognize initial sounds in words by prolonging or stretching pronunciation of initial sounds of words or iterating (repeating several times—especially for sounds that include intrusive vowels) the initial sounds of words.

2. Have children practice this skill by matching a sound with a picture of an object that produces that sound when read. For instance, say /b/ and have the children attempt to match it with a picture of a ball.

3. Have children practice identifying the initial sounds in words by reading them words and asking them what sound each word starts with.

The tasks identified above would be most appropriate at the readiness level (kindergarten to first grade). Other activities that extend and expand those outlined above are discussed in Chapter 5.

VISUAL DISCRIMINATION

Children develop their ability to discriminate visually as they explore their environment through a combination of tactile and visual approaches. Spache & Spache (1986) point out that children who lack experiences with objects or forms at near-point range often have difficulty with reading.

Since reading is a visual act and requires visual discrimination ability, teachers should prepare children for phonics by providing exercises that help them discriminate between letters and words. Research results indicate that this task is best accomplished by having children practice using letters and words rather than pictures or various geometric shapes (Durkin, 1993).

Visual Discrimination Exercises

Visual discrimination exercises should progress in a logical sequence from simple to complex. Below are sequenced examples of exercises that can be used to further develop visual discrimination skills. Beyond these examples, teachers should be able to develop additional activities for improving visual discrimination.

Activity 1: *Matching letters.* In this example, the student circles the letter on each line that is identical to the first letter of that line. (Examples progress from simple to complex.)

t — s	w	t	o
O — T	O	V	X
w — m	n	w	u
b — d	b	p	q

As students are able to successfully complete simple letter discriminations, more complex discriminations should be developed and administered. (This also holds true for the exercises that follow.)

Additional variations: Develop and write out two *game-type* variations that will provide practice in single-letter discrimination. A sample is provided.

1. Card matching: Construct a deck of 52 cards consisting of duplicate small letters. All 52 cards are placed face down. Children take turns flipping over two cards. If the cards match, the student keeps them. The game ends when all of the cards have been paired up. The winner is the child with the most cards. This game can be varied by using only consonant letters, vowel letters, or limiting the number of matching cards used in the game.

2. _____
   _____
   _____
   _____
   _____

3. _____
   _____
   _____
   _____
   _____

Activity 2: *Matching double letters.* In this example, the student circles the pair of letters on each line that is identical to the first two letters of that line. (Examples progress from simple to complex.)

ok — ts   xy   ok   mn

SP	— OT	SP	MA	UW
ab	— ap	ab	ba	pa
MN	— NM	WN	MN	MW

Additional variations: Develop and write out two *game-type* variations that will provide practice in double-letter discrimination. (Develop variations that are different from your single-letter game-type variations.)

1. _____

_____

_____

_____

_____

2. _____

_____

_____

_____

_____

Activity 3:   *Matching words.* In this example, the student circles the word on each line that is identical to the first word of that line. (Examples progress from simple to complex.)

big	— car	big	was	ran
TOP	— CAR	SAW	TOP	BAG
boy	— big	bay	bag	boy
dog	— god	dog	bog	dot

Additional variations: Develop and write out two *game-type* variations that will provide practice in small-word discrimination. (Again, develop variations that differ from your single- and double-letter variations.)

1. _____

_____

_____

_____

2. _____

_____

_____

_____

AUDITORY DISCRIMINATION

Children must be able to hear likenesses among and differences between sounds as they occur in spoken words. This ability or skill is known as auditory discrimination. A typical auditory discrimination test would ask children to recognize the fine differences between the phonemes used in English speech. For instance, children might be asked to say whether word pairs that are read to them sound exactly the same or different. Minimal word pairs that differ by a single phoneme in the beginning position (hot-cot), middle position (met-mit), and ending position (sad-sat) are used with word pairs that are identical (man-man) to measure this skill. One study (Spache, Andres, Curtis, Rowland, & Fields, 1965) attempting to predict first-grade reading success based on tests of visual discrimination, auditory discrimination, and auditory vocabulary found that measures of auditory discrimination were the best overall predictors. These results suggest that auditory discrimination is a significant factor in beginning reading.

It must be remembered that measures of auditory discrimination provide only partial data when differentiating between children who need training and children who do not. In using auditory discrimination data, the following considerations should be kept in mind: poor performance may, in fact, reflect a hearing loss rather than a lack of auditory discrimination. In addition, some speech sounds are often not mastered by the age of 6 or 7 (Spache & Spache, 1986). These limitations, however, do not render auditory discrimination measures worthless. If the test results are used with limitations in mind and complemented by other pertinent data (i.e., teacher observations, classroom achievement, medical information), auditory discrimination measures can provide valuable input regarding a child's readiness to use phonics in learning to read.

Auditory Awareness Exercises

Since oral language serves as the foundation on which reading skills are built, teachers should provide children with numerous experiences in both listening and speech. Activities similar to those listed below will allow children to "work" with language in a productive way.

Activity 1: Read to children daily. Nursery rhymes and rhyming books provide children with opportunities to experience similar sounds in a patterned manner.

Activity 2: Storybook reading provides opportunities for listening, but should also provide children with meaningful opportunities for using oral language.

Activity 3:   Have children identify the sounds heard in the classroom and around the school.

Activity 4:   Have children close their eyes, then ask them to identify the sounds of snapping fingers, a pencil sharpener, tearing paper, chalkboard writing, etc.

Activity 5:   Play recordings of common sounds and have children identify them.

Activity 6:   Have children play a game in which they have to identify sounds made by a child who imitates a sound from a specific place, such as a farm, airport, highway, zoo, etc.

Auditory Discrimination Exercises

To provide more direct opportunities to improve auditory discrimination skills, you must have children work with the sounds of the English language, not simply sounds in general, as was done while building auditory awareness in the examples above. In addition, it is important for children to either hear someone else voicing the sounds or say the sounds themselves *out loud*. Too often auditory discrimination activities require children to identify the sounds, as represented by pictures, silently as they make decisions about likenesses and differences, rather than having them name the pictures out loud. Activities can be used to provide practice in beginning, middle, and ending sounds. The instructor should introduce beginning sounds first, followed by ending sounds, and finally, middle sounds. Although the following activities are designed to practice beginning-sound discrimination, they can be modified to include work on the endings and middles of words as well.

Activity 1:   Read word pairs to the class (cot-hot; man-man; sin-pin; etc.). Ask if they begin with the same sound or a different sound. Always keep in mind that the language used to instruct must be understood by students. If, in this case, they did not know what "same" or "different" meant, the strategy has no value.

Activity 2:   Have children listen to a series of words that begin with the same consonant sound. Ask children to identify other words that begin with the same sound.

Activity 3:   Read a series of words to children (e.g., cat, come, cane, man), have the entire class repeat all the words together, and ask them to say the one that does not belong.

Activity 4:   Provide beginning sounds for the children (e.g., /s/) and ask them to say words that begin with the same sounds.

Activity 5:   Introduce children to rhyming words through the use of nursery rhymes and poetry.

Develop and write two specific rhyming activities that enhance the development of auditory discrimination. A sample is provided.

1. In the two sentences, "I have a cat" and "He is very fat," can you identify the words that rhyme? I am going to read two more sentences, but this time I am going to leave out the last word in the second sentence. See if you can think of and say a word that rhymes with the last word of the first sentence. "I know a girl named Jill." "She went to the doctor to get a _____." (pill)

2. _____

   _____

   _____

   _____

   _____

   _____

   _____

3. _____

   _____

   _____

   _____

   _____

   _____

LETTER NAMES

To provide effective readiness instruction, teachers must understand the type of relationship that exists between knowledge of letter names and learning to read.

A number of research studies have shown that letter knowledge is not necessarily a prerequisite for learning to read. On the other hand numerous studies have also shown that children who begin their schooling with a knowledge of the ABC's are more likely to become better readers than children who lack this knowledge. For some time this was taken to mean that letter knowledge was helpful or necessary in learning to read. Most authorities now agree, however, that knowledge of the ABC's, for entering school aged children, is simply indicative of a host of factors that are often conducive to learning to read. Among these factors are a natural potential for learning to read, educational level of [the student's] parents, and [a] good reading environment at home (Ekwall, 1976, p. 64).

Therefore, the readiness instruction in letter names for phonics must not be done under the false assumption that it will *cause* children to become good readers. Rather, it should be understood that children's knowledge of letter names will enable the teacher to communicate more effectively with them as instruction occurs.

MEASURING VISUAL AND AUDITORY DISCRIMINATION

Numerous standardized tests measure visual and/or auditory discrimination. It is important to note that there are reference books available in which teachers can find evaluative information regarding the strengths and weaknesses of standardized tests. Teachers who are faced with the important decision of selecting such instruments should consult the latest *Mental Measurement Yearbook*, edited by Jane Close Conoley and James C. Impara (twelfth yearbook is the most recent).

EMERGENT LITERACY

Although most attention to readiness factors has been placed in the context of formal schooling, the encounters that children have with reading and writing before formal schooling begins have become increasingly important in understanding how children learn to read. Sulzby & Teale (1991) explain emergent literacy as follows:

> Emergent literacy is concerned with the earliest phases of literacy development, the period between birth and the time when children read and write conventionally. The term *emergent literacy* signals a belief that, in a literate society, young children—even 1- and 2-year-olds—are in the process of becoming literate. This literacy is seen in not-yet-conventional behaviors; underlying the behaviors are understandings or hypotheses about literacy. Literacy learning is seen as taking place in home and community settings, in out-of-home care settings, and in school settings such as Head Start, prekindergarten, and kindergarten (p. 728).

Thus, it is important for teachers to realize that the wide range of experiences that children have had with language before formal school begins should be used in assisting them to learn to read. Children's understanding about print awareness, concepts of print, sense of story, oral language, and writing will have a significant bearing on their ultimate success in reading achievement.

■ ■ ■ **CHAPTER 4: PRACTICE**

Survey one current basal reading series to ascertain the importance of the roles that visual discrimination and auditory discrimination play in preparing children for phonics instruction. Respond to the following questions.

1. Who was the publisher of the basal reading series that you selected? What year was it published?

_____

_____

_____

2. At what level (grade) are visual discrimination activities introduced?

_____

_____

_____

3. At what level (grade) are auditory discrimination activities introduced?

_____

_____

_____

4. At what levels (grades) does most of the visual discrimination instruction occur? Where does formal instruction in this area appear to end?

_____

_____

_____

5. At what levels (grades) does most of the auditory discrimination instruction occur? When does formal instruction in this area appear to end?

_____

_____

_____

6. Identify and write out three visual discrimination activities presented in the basal text.
   a. _____

   _____

   _____

   _____

   _____

b. _____
_____
_____
_____
_____
_____

c. _____
_____
_____
_____
_____

7. Identify and write out three auditory discrimination activities presented in the basal text.

a. _____
_____
_____
_____
_____
_____

b. _____
_____
_____
_____
_____

c. _____
_____
_____
_____
_____

8. Construct a short test of visual discrimination. If possible, administer the test to a child of age 4 to 6. What were your findings? What difficulties did you or the child encounter?

_____
_____
_____
_____
_____

_____

_____

_____

9. Consult the latest *Mental Measurement Yearbook* and select a reading readiness test to review. Write out the test's strengths and weaknesses as identified by the expert(s) critiquing it.

_____

_____

_____

_____

_____

_____

_____

_____

10. What implications does the concept of emergent literacy hold for teachers of beginning reading?

_____

_____

_____

_____

_____

_____

_____

_____

_____

_____

_____

_____

_____

■ ■ ■ **CUMULATIVE REVIEW OF CHAPTERS 1 THROUGH 4**

1. A _____ is a part of the syllable that includes the vowel sound and any consonant sound(s) that come after it.

2. A *single vowel sound* made up of a glide from one vowel to another in immediate sequence and pronounced in one syllable is called a _____.

3. A *phonogram* is the graphic representation of a _____.

4. Any syllable that ends with a vowel phoneme is called a(n) _____ syllable.

5. The sounds represented by *bl* in *blue* are called a _____.

6. A _____ is a soft vowel sound closely resembling the short sound of *u* that commonly occurs in unstressed syllables.

7. The _____ is a symbol placed over a vowel letter to show it is pronounced as a short sound.

8. The phoneme /oi/ is an example of a _____.

9. (True–False) All digraphs are graphemes.
   (True–False) All graphemes are digraphs.

10. If a child enters kindergarten reading at the third-grade level, do you believe that she should go through the phonics curriculum as set up by the district? Why?

_____

_____

_____

_____

_____

_____

_____

_____

_____

_____

_____

11. Define the following phonic terms.

Phoneme: _____

_____

_____

Grapheme: _____

_____

_____

Digraph: _____

_____

_____

Onset: _____

_____

_____

12. Identify and discuss three factors that could have an impact on a child's ability to learn to read successfully.

    a. _____

    _____

    _____

    _____

    _____

    b. _____

    _____

    _____

    _____

    _____

    c. _____

    _____

    _____

    _____

    _____

5

■ ■ ■ ■ ■

Phonemes

As discussed earlier, phonemes are the smallest sound units of a language that distinguish one word from another. There are 44 phonemes in the English language; 25 of these are consonant phonemes and 19 are vowel phonemes. The fact that there are over 200 different ways to spell the 44 phonemes creates confusion when learning how to read or spell in English.

CONSONANT PHONEMES—PRONUNCIATION KEY

Single letters (there are 18): Each word below represents the most common spelling of an initial consonant sound.

/b/	bat
/d/	did
/f/	fat
/g/	go
/h/	he
/j/	jam
/k/	come
/l/	let
/m/	me
/n/	no
/p/	pan
/r/	run
/s/	sat
/t/	ten
/v/	very

/w/   w̲ill
/y/   y̲es
/z/   z̲oo

Letters *c*, *q*, and *x* do not represent phonemes that are identified by their own name. Instead, these sound units are identified with like-sounding phonemes from the list above:

c represents the phonemes we associate with /s/ in *cent* or /k/ in *coat.*

q represents the phonemes we associate with /k/ /w/ in *quit* or /k/ in *antique.*

x represents the phonemes we associate with /g/ /z/ in *exit*, /k/ /s/ in *sox*, or /z/ in *xylophone.*

Double Letters (there are 7):

/ch/   c̲h̲air
/hw/   w̲h̲y
/ng/   son̲g̲
/sh/   s̲h̲e
/th/   t̲h̲in
/TH/   t̲h̲at
/zh/   mea̲s̲ure

VOWEL PHONEMES—PRONUNCIATION KEY

Each word listed below represents the most common spelling of vowel phonemes.

Long Vowels:

/ā/   a̲ge
/ē/   ea̲se
/ī/   i̲ce
/ō/   o̲ld
/ū/   u̲se

Short Vowels:

/ă/   a̲n
/ĕ/   e̲nd
/ĭ/   i̲n

/ŏ/   odd

/ŭ/   up

Diphthongs:

/oi/   oil boy

/ou/   out owl

Double o:

/o͞o/   too rule

/o͝o/   good pudding

Others:

/ä/   star, father

/â/   dare, air

/û/   her, pearl

/ô/   order, auto, off, tall

When vowel letters are followed by an r, they are known as r-controlled. This results in a sound that is neither short nor long.

Schwa /ə/:

a as in *about, senator*

o as in *occur, lemon*

e as in *effect, open*

i as in *pencil, notify*

u as in *circus, insulate*

au as in *authority*

ai as in *mountain*

ou as in *famous*

ea as in *pageant*

eo as in *dungeon*

oi as in *tortoise*

PHONEMIC AWARENESS

As discussed earlier in Chapter 4, a high correlation exists between reading achievement and the ability to recognize spoken words as a sequence of individual sounds. It has been shown that explicit instruction can increase one's phonemic awareness (Lewkowicz, 1980). To expand and extend the beginning skills of segmentation and blending as presented in Chapter 4, the following activities are offered.

44 **44**   Chapter 5

Activity 1—Phoneme Segmentation: Phoneme segmentation is the ability to isolate all the sounds of a word. Nation & Hulme (1997) found in their research that "phonemic segmentation is an excellent predictor of reading and spelling skill, even in the early stages of literacy development" (p. 166). In teaching this skill, Lewkowicz (1980) found that it is extremely important for the teacher to prolong or stretch the word to be segmented and essential that the child attend to the articulatory clues, as well as the auditory clues, by slowly pronouncing the word.

1. Introduce children to the concept through modeling: slowly saying a word and emphasizing its sounds; then identifying each sound separately. For instance, read *dog* slowly and then identify /d/ /ô/ /g/ as its three sounds.

2. Provide practice for children by slowly reading words to them, emphasizing each sound. Ask children to articulate the individual sounds that make up each word. Start with two-letter words and advance from there to longer words as children become competent in voicing each sound in the words. At first, it is also effective to help the student by identifying the number of sounds in each word. As students gain the ability to segment words, the number of sounds can be withheld.

Activity 2—Phoneme Counting: Ask children to count the number of sounds they hear as you read words slowly. Start with two-letter words and advance from there. Gradually reduce the slowness of pronunciation as children gain proficiency in this skill.

Activity 3—Phoneme Blending: Blending is the process of recognizing isolated speech sounds and the ability to pronounce the word for which they stand when combined. The most appropriate time to "introduce blending seems likely to be when children have just 'gotten the hang of' segmentation and are practicing it intensively" (Lewkowicz, 1980, p. 697).

1. Have children practice blending two-phoneme words segmented into two parts (i.e., /n/ /ō/).

2. Have children practice blending three- or four-phoneme words segmented into two parts (i.e., /r/–/ă/ /t/; /s/ /t/–/ŏ/ /p/).

3. Advance to having children practice blending three- or four-phoneme words segmented into three parts (i.e., /d/–/ô/–/g/; /t/ /r/–/ĭ/–/p/.

Activity 4—Phoneme Deletion: This activity requires children to identify a new word that is made when a phoneme is deleted from the original word.

1. Read a word to the children and have them pronounce the word that would result if they were to leave off the first sound. For example, they

might be asked to say *sat* with the /s/ deleted. This activity may be more effective if the leftover words are also real words.

2. This activity can be extended to include ending and medial sounds only after students become confident in their ability to deal with beginning sounds.

Activity 5—Phoneme Substitution: Replace an identified sound with a new one and pronounce the new word. For instance, in the word *seat*, if you replace the /s/ with a /b/, how would the new word be pronounced? (A similar activity is often used in school where children are asked to identify new words through letter substitution rather than through sound substitution. It is suggested here that more work needs to be done with sound substitutions.)

Activity 6—Identification of Deleted Phonemes: This activity is similar to Activity 4 above because it relates to a deleted phoneme. In this activity, however, children are asked to identify the missing phoneme when comparing two similar sounding words. For instance, what sound do you hear in *mat* that is not in *at*?

■ ■ ■   **CHAPTER 5: PRACTICE**

1. There are _____ phonemes in the English language, _____ consonant phonemes and _____ vowel phonemes.
2. The schwa sound usually has a(n) (consistent, inconsistent) spelling. (Circle one.)
3. The inconsistent spelling of (consonant sounds, vowel sounds) is a basic problem of phonics. (Circle one.)
4. Check the pair(s) below that contain(s) the same vowel phoneme.
   a. book—room   _____
   b. wool—food   _____
   c. pool—stood   _____
   d. too—shoes   _____
5. Check each word below that contains a diphthong.
   a. coil   _____
   b. out   _____
   c. own   _____
   d. owl   _____
   e. could   _____
6. The letters _____, _____, and _____ do not represent phonemes that are identified by their own name.

7. Fill in the proper consonant phoneme for each of the underlined letter(s).

center   / /   seizure   / /

chrome   / /   graph   / /

know   / /   germ   / /

sure   / /   whom   / /

wrong   / /   ghost   / /

white   / /   antique   / /

8. Fill in the proper vowel phoneme for each of the underlined letter(s).

paid   / /   turn   / /

die   / /   plaid   / /

boy   / /   owl   / /

eulogy   / /   pull   / /

wand   / /   said   / /

rule   / /   other   / /

9. How many phonemes are represented in the following words? Write each word using its phoneme pronunciation symbols.

sight   ___3___   /s/ /ī/ /t/

sew   _____   _____

sing   _____   _____

blue   _____   _____

ghost   _____   _____

ship   _____   _____

old   _____   _____

boy   _____   _____

bird   _____   _____

both   _____   _____

box   _____   _____

cent   _____   _____

comb   _____   _____

cow   _____   _____

low   _____   _____

■ ■ ■   **CUMULATIVE REVIEW OF CHAPTERS 1 THROUGH 5**

1. List two reasons why teachers should provide opportunities for children to learn and use all word-recognition methods.

_____

_____

_____

_____

_____

_____

_____

_____

2. (Phonics, Phonetics) is the method used to teach beginning reading. (Circle one.)

3. A closed syllable ends with a _____ _____.

4. A letter or combination of letters that represents a phoneme is called a _____.

5. (True–False) Implicit approaches to teaching phonics have proven more effective than explicit approaches.

6. A _____ is a unit of pronunciation that consists of a vowel alone or a vowel with one or more consonants.

7. An unstressed sound commonly occurring in unstressed syllables and very closely resembling the short _u_ sound is a _____.

8. Reading is a visual act that requires effective _____ vision.

9. _____ _____, the ability to hear sounds of varying pitch and loudness, is an important factor in beginning reading.

10. (True–False) Children who enter school with a knowledge of letter names are more likely to become better readers than children who lack this knowledge. Therefore, teaching children the letter names in kindergarten should eliminate many of our reading problems at the lower grade levels. Why?

_____

_____

_____

_____

11. Research indicates that practicing visual discrimination for reading is best accomplished through what kind of activities?

_____

_____

_____
_____
_____
_____
_____

12. Provide a word that contains each of the following:

    Vowel digraph: _____

    Consonant digraph: _____

    Diphthong: _____

    Schwa: _____

    Blend: _____

    Open syllable: _____

    Closed syllable: _____

13. If you wanted an expert opinion about the strengths and weaknesses of a particular standardized test, what source would be an excellent starting point?

    _____

14. How many phonemes are represented in the following words? Write each word using its phoneme pronunciation symbols.

    plum   __4__   /p/ /l/ /ŭ/ /m/

    off   _____   _____

    future   _____   _____

    naked   _____   _____

    true   _____   _____

    plume   _____   _____

    funny   _____   _____

    queen   _____   _____

    mix   _____   _____

    hare   _____   _____

6

■ ■ ■ ■ ■

Phonic Generalizations

Much has been written about the utility of phonic generalizations over the past 35 years. Although some work in the area had been accomplished before 1960, an article by Clymer (1963) questioning the appropriateness of the many phonic generalizations taught at the time gave rise to several research projects designed to examine and extend what Clymer studied.

In essence, Clymer analyzed the instructor's manuals of four widely used primary grade readers and identified 121 generalizations: 50 vowel generalizations, 15 consonant generalizations, 28 ending generalizations, and 28 syllabication generalizations. Of these, 45 generalizations were selected arbitrarily for further study (each had to be specific enough to be applied to individual words). A list of 2,600 words was developed by combining the words introduced in the four readers with the words from the Gates Reading Vocabulary for the Primary Grades. Using Webster's *New Collegiate Dictionary* as the pronunciation authority, each applicable word was checked against the appropriate generalization. From this check, a "percent of utility" was computed for each generalization. For instance, if 10 words could be applied to a generalization, 5 of which followed the generalization and 5 of which did not, the generalization would have a 50 percent utility.

At the beginning of the study, Clymer postulated that a 75 percent utility was indicative of a useful generalization. Only 18 of the 45 generalizations satisfied this utility criterion (Table 1, pp. 50–53). The results of Clymer's study proved disturbing to him and others because they ran counter to what many instructors had been teaching for many years.

Clymer's research was followed by other studies on similar aspects of phonic generalizations. Bailey (1967) examined the 45 phonic generalizations studied previously by Clymer but extended the word list to include all words in the student textbooks from eight basal reading series, grades 1 through 6. She concluded that only 6 generalizations (Clymer's

TABLE 1 The Utility for 45 Phonic Generalizations (pp. 50–53)

Generalization	No. of Words Conforming	No. of Exceptions	Percent of Utility
1. When there are two vowels side by side, the long sound of the first is heard and the second is usually silent.	309 (bead)**	377 (chief)	45
2. When a vowel is in the middle of a one-syllable word, the vowel is short.	408	249	62
Middle letter	191 (dress)	84 (scold)	69
One of the middle two letters in a word of four letters	191 (rest)	135 (told)	59
One vowel within a word of more than four letters	26 (splash)	30 (fight)	46
3. If the only vowel letter is at the end of a word, the letter usually stands for a long sound.	23 (he)	8 (to)	74
4. When there are two vowels, one of which is a final e, the first vowel is long and the e is silent.	180 (bone)	108 (done)	63
*5. The r gives the preceding vowel a sound that is neither long nor short.	184 (horn)	134 (wire)	78
6. The first vowel is usually long and the second silent in the digraphs ai, ea, oa, and ui.	179	92	66
ai	43 (nail)	24 (said)	64
ea	101 (bead)	51 (head)	66
oa	34 (boat)	1 (cupboard)	97
ui	1 (suit)	16 (build)	6
7. In the phonogram ie, the i is silent and the e has a long sound.	8 (field)	39 (friend)	17
*8. Words having double e usually have the long e sound.	85 (seem)	2 (been)	98
9. When words end with silent e, the preceding a or i is long.	164 (cake)	108 (have)	60

No.	Generalization			Percent
*10.	In ay the y is silent and gives a its long sound.	36 (play)	10 (always)	78
11.	When the letter i is followed by the letters gh, the i usually stands for its long sound and the gh is silent.	22 (high)	9 (neighbor)	71
12.	When a follows w in a word, it usually has the sound a as in was.	15 (watch)	32 (swam)	32
13.	When e is followed by w, the vowel sound is the same as represented by oo.	9 (blew)	17 (sew)	35
14.	The two letters ow make the long o sound.	50 (own)	35 (down)	59
15.	W is sometimes a vowel and follows the vowel digraph rule.	50 (crow)	75 (threw)	40
*16.	When y is the final letter in a word, it usually has a vowel sound.	169 (dry)	32 (tray)	84
17.	When y is used as a vowel in words, it sometimes has the sound of long i.	29 (fly)	170 (funny)	15
18.	The letter a has the same sound (o) when followed by l, w, and u.	61 (all)	65 (canal)	48
19.	When a is followed by r and final e, we expect to hear the sound heard in care.	9 (dare)	1 (are)	90
*20.	When c and h are next to each other, they make only one sound.	103 (peach)	0	100
*21.	Ch is usually pronounced as it is in kitchen, catch, and chair, not like sh.	99 (catch)	5 (machine)	95
*22.	When c is followed by e or i, the sound of s is likely to be heard.	66 (cent)	3 (ocean)	96
*23.	When the letter c is followed by o or a, the sound of k is likely to be heard.	143 (camp)	0	100
24.	The letter g often has a sound similar to that of j in jump when it precedes the letter i or e.	49 (engine)	28 (give)	64
*25.	When ght is seen in a word; gh is silent.	30 (fight)	0	100

*Generalizations marked with an asterisk were found "useful" according to the criteria.
**Words in parentheses are examples—either of words that conform or of exceptions, depending on the column.

TABLE 1 (continued)

Generalization	No. of Words Conforming	No. of Exceptions	Percent of Utility
26. When a word begins with kn, the k is silent.	10 (knife)**	0	100
27. When a word begins with wr, the w is silent.	8 (write)	0	100
*28. When two of the same consonants are side by side, only one is heard.	334 (carry)	3 (suggest)	99
*29. When a word ends in ck, it has the same last sound as in look.	46 (brick)	0	100
*30. In most two-syllable words, the first syllable is accented.	828 (famous)	143 (polite)	85
*31. If a, in, re, ex, de, or be is the first syllable in a word, it is usually unaccented.	86 (belong)	13 (insect)	87
*32. In most two-syllable words that end in a consonant followed by a y, the first syllable is accented and the last is unaccented.	101 (baby)	4 (supply)	96
33. One vowel letter in an accented syllable has its short sound.	547 (city)	356 (lady)	61
34. When y or ey is seen in the last syllable that is not accented, the long sound of e is heard.	0	157 (baby)	0
35. When ture is the final syllable in a word, it is unaccented.	4 (picture)	0	100
36. When tion is the final syllable in a word, it is unaccented.	5 (station)	0	100
37. In many two- and three-syllable words, the final e lengthens the vowel in the last syllable.	52 (invite)	62 (gasoline)	46
38. If the first vowel sound in a word is followed by two consonants, the first syllable usually ends with the first of the two consonants.	404 (bullet)	159 (singer)	72
39. If the first vowel sound in a word is followed by a single consonant, that consonant usually begins the second syllable.	190 (over)	237 (oven)	44

52

No.	Generalization	Number Conforming	Number of Exceptions	Percent of Utility
*40.	If the last syllable of a word ends in le, the consonant preceding the le usually begins the last syllable.	62 (tumble)	2 (buckle)	97
*41.	When the first vowel element in a word is followed by th, ch, or sh, these symbols are not broken when the word is divided into syllables and may go with either the first or second syllable.	30 (dishes)	0	100
42.	In a word of more than one syllable, the letter v usually goes with the preceding vowel to form a syllable.	53 (cover)	20 (clover)	73
43.	When a word has only one vowel letter, the vowel sound is likely to be short.	433 (hid)	322 (kind)	57
*44.	When there is one e in a word that ends in a consonant, the e usually has a short sound.	85 (leg)	27 (blew)	76
*45.	When the last syllable is the sound r, it is unaccented.	188 (butter)	9 (appear)	95

*Generalizations marked with an asterisk were found "useful" according to the criteria.
**Words in parentheses are examples—either of words that conform or of exceptions, depending on the column.
Source: Reprinted with permission of Ted Clymer and the International Reading Association.

numbers 20, 22, 23, 28, 32, and 40 in Table 1) "were found to be simple to understand and apply, to be applicable to large numbers of words, and to have few exceptions" (p. 414). Emans (1967), using the same generalizations and procedures as Clymer, studied words beyond the primary level (grade 4) to determine the usefulness of phonic generalizations. He found that 16 of the 45 generalizations (Clymer's 5, 8, 16, 20, 22, 23, 24, 28, 30, 31, 32, 36, 38, 40, 41, and 45) met the criteria established by Clymer. Other studies by Burmeister (1968); Caldwell, Roth, & Turner (1978); Fuld (1968); Gates (1986); and Hillerich (1978) have addressed various aspects of phonic generalizations. Based on the results of those studies and an examination of current basal series, certain consonant and vowel generalizations stand out as having enough utility to be of value in phonics instruction.

CONSONANT GENERALIZATIONS

Consonant generalizations are more consistent than vowel generalizations. The following appear to offer the most instructional value:

1. *c* usually represents the "soft c" as in *cent* and *race* when followed by the letters *e, i,* or *y*. Otherwise, the *c* usually represents the "hard c" as in *coat* and *cot*.

2. *g* usually represents the "soft g" as in *gym* and *wage* when followed by the letters *e, i,* and *y*. Otherwise, the *g* usually represents the "hard g" as in *go* and *nag*.

When using the two generalizations above, children should be taught that there are exceptions. If, when attempting to identify a word, they find that the generalization does not appear to work, children should be encouraged to try the other sound before seeking help.

3. The consonant digraph *ch* is usually pronounced /ch/ as in *church*, but may also represent the sounds of /k/ as in *chemical*, or /sh/ as in *machine*.

4. When identical consonant letters are next to each other, only one is usually heard, as in *letter, call,* and *cannon*.

5. Certain consonant letters represent more than one sound. (See also 1 and 2 above.)

s		*x*	
smile	/s/	anxiety	/z/
is	/z/	mix	/k/ /s/
sure	/sh/	exit	/g/ /z/
pleasure	/zh/		

6. When a word ends in *ck*, it has the sound /k/ as in *book*.
7. When a word begins with *kn*, the *k* is silent, as in *knit*.
8. When a word begins with *wr*, the *w* is silent, as in *wrong*.
9. When a word begins with *gn*, the *g* is silent, as in *gnat*.

VOWEL GENERALIZATIONS

Although the correspondence between vowel letters and sounds in English is less consistent than the correspondence between consonant letters and sounds, some consistency does exist and allows for the following vowel generalizations:

1. A single vowel letter in a syllable usually represents the short sound if it is not the final letter (cat, but, lot, met, mit).
2. A single vowel letter in a syllable usually represents the long sound if it is the final letter (he, hi, go, pa–per, ti–ger).
3. When two vowel letters in a syllable are separated by a consonant and one is a final *e*, the first usually records its long sound and the *e* is silent (hope, late, cute).
4. When two successive vowel letters occur in a syllable and they are not any of the special digraphs (oi, oy, ow, ou, oo, au), the first vowel letter is usually long and the second silent (especially ee—keep, ea—meat, ai—pain, ay—say, oa—load).

Because there are many exceptions to the above generalizations, Spache and Spache (1986) recommend that children should learn to use a systematic approach when meeting an unknown word. If the sound of the first letter or blend combined with context is not sufficient to "unlock" the word, a closer look at vowels is suggested. An application of appropriate vowel generalizations (see 1 to 4 above) is used in the next attempt at correct pronunciation. If the vowel generalization fails, the other vowel sound should be attempted. Should these efforts fail, assistance from a dictionary or teacher would then be appropriate.

This systematic approach emphasizes that generalizations are only guidelines. When they do not work, other sounds should be attempted.

5. *ow* has two sounds, the /ō/ as in *own* and the /ou/ as in *cow*.
6. *oo* has two sounds, the /o͞o/ as in *food* and the /o͝o/ as in *foot*.
7. The *r* gives the vowel before it a sound that is neither long nor short.
8. The vowel digraphs *oi, oy, ou*, and *ow* blend into a single sound (diphthong) as in *boil, boy, out, owl*.
9. *y* at the end of a word usually represents a vowel sound.

In teaching the above generalizations, two approaches may be taken. One procedure would center on the teacher telling children about generalizations and having them apply those generalizations to specific words. This telling process is known as *deductive* instruction. For instance, a generalization like the following is taught first, "When there are two vowels side by side, the long sound of the first is heard and the second is silent." Children are then asked to apply it to specific examples.

A second procedure would be described as *inductive*. The inductive process begins with specifics and moves to generalizations about them. For instance, children might be asked to analyze the vowels in a group of words (*boat, heat, rain, low*), from which they will identify a common characteristic and ultimately develop a generalization to cover the pattern (first vowel long and second vowel silent).

Both approaches have their place in phonics instruction. For instance, inductive instruction provides children with opportunities for developing strategies of independent learning. On the other hand, deductive instruction has certain time advantages and can be used when efficient use of time becomes an important element in the teaching situation. In addition, not all children have success with the inductive approach. Consequently, a combination of the two processes can serve a valuable function in phonics instruction.

■ ■ ■ CHAPTER 6: PRACTICE

1. An analysis of Clymer's 1963 study reveals that _____ generalizations generally have a greater utility value than do _____ generalizations.
2. Circle the following nonsense words in which *c* would most likely represent the "soft c" sound.
   cint   cule   cymp   sluce
3. The consonant digraph *ch* usually represents the phoneme /__/. However, it may also represent the phonemes /__/ and /__/.
4. When identical consonant letters are next to each other, (both, only one) (are, is) usually heard. (Circle one of each.)
5. (Deductive, Inductive) teaching begins with specifics and moves to generalizations. It is analytic in nature. (Circle one.)
6. Circle the following nonsense words in which *g* would most likely represent the "hard g" sound.
   giltion   gultion   buge   seg
7. When a word begins with *kn*, the *k* is _____.

8. When the _____ _____ ck ends a word
   it represents the phoneme /__/.

The following questions should be answered using the vowel generalization information presented earlier. Each question will require the vowel pronunciation contained in a nonsense word. Circle the correct answer.

9. The *e* in *slek* has the same sound as:
   a. *e* in *he.*
   b. *e* in *err.*
   c. *e* in *end.*
   d. *e* in *her.*
   e. none of the above.

10. The *a* in *swa* has the same sound as:
   a. *a* in *may.*
   b. *a* in *wand.*
   c. *a* in *add.*
   d. *a* in *art.*
   e. none of the above.

11. The *o* in *kote* has the same sound as:
   a. *o* in *cop.*
   b. *o* in *orange.*
   c. *o* in *go.*
   d. *o* in *out.*
   e. none of the above.

12. The *e* in *ceab* has the same sound as:
   a. *e* in *he.*
   b. *e* in *err.*
   c. *e* in *end.*
   d. *e* in *her.*
   e. none of the above.

13. The *o* in *woab* has the same sound as:
   a. *o* in *boy.*
   b. *o* in *go.*
   c. *o* in *out.*
   d. *o* in *cot.*
   e. none of the above.

14. The *u* in *knupe* has the same sound as:
   a. *u* in *up.*
   b. *u* in *run.*
   c. *u* in *hurt.*
   d. *u* in *use.*
   e. none of the above.

15. The *i* in *fif* has the same sound as:
    a. *i* in *high*.
    b. *i* in *girl*.
    c. *i* in *in*.
    d. *i* in *pine*.
    e. none of the above.
16. The *a* in *paic* has the same sound as:
    a. *a* in *art*.
    b. *a* in *name*.
    c. *a* in *map*.
    d. *a* in *swan*.
    e. none of the above.
17. A single vowel letter in a syllable usually represents the short sound if
    _____.
18. A single vowel letter in a syllable usually represents the long sound if
    _____.
19. When two vowel letters in a syllable are separated by a consonant and one is a final *e*, the first usually records its _____ sound and the *e* is _____.
20. When two successive vowel letters occur in a syllable and they are not any of the special digraphs, the first usually records its _____ sound and the second is _____.

■ ■ ■ CUMULATIVE REVIEW OF CHAPTERS 1 THROUGH 6

1. (True–False) It appears that a commitment to whole-word instruction is in direct opposition to using a phonics approach in any significant way.
2. The study of human speech sounds is called _____.
3. A _____ is the symbol used to represent a long vowel sound.
4. There is only one _____ phoneme in each syllable.
5. A phoneme is the _____ sound unit of a language that distinguishes one word from another.
6. The *oa* in *boat* is called a _____.
7. _____ _____ is the ability to hear likenesses and differences among sounds as they occur in spoken words.
8. Readiness to read (is, is not) something that exists in an absolute sense. (Circle one.) Why?
    _____

_____

_____

_____

9. In the words below, indicate the vowel phoneme represented by each underlined letter or pair of letters.

dance   /__/   awful   /__/

double /__/   away   /__/

put   /__/   avenge /__/

disk   /__/   verse   /__/

10. In the words below, indicate the consonant phoneme represented by each underlined letter or pair of letters.

gym   /__/   why   /__/

goat   /__/   phone   /__/

coat   /__/   sox   /__/ /__/

who   /__/   cent   /__/

11. How many phonemes are represented in the following words? Write each word using its phoneme pronunciation symbols.

phone   _____   _____

out   _____   _____

knew   _____   _____

about   _____   _____

auto   _____   _____

could   _____   _____

toy   _____   _____

pearl   _____   _____

pudding _____   _____

dare   _____   _____

7

■ ■ ■ ■ ■

Teaching Consonants and Vowels

The most current basal reading series generally include a significant amount of phonics training at the lower levels. An examination of the phonics content of current basal series leads to several observations:

1. The scope and sequence of phonics in basal series vary widely, and research has not identified the best sequence in which decoding skills should be taught. Consequently, decisions about the order of instruction are often related to the words used in the basal series' stories.

2. Formal instruction begins with an emphasis on initial consonant sounds. This practice appears logical because (a) consonant sounds are more consistent in their spelling than are vowel sounds and so are less confusing to children, (b) written English has a left-to-right orientation whereby the initial position of words assumes the most significant position in word recognition, and (c) most of the words children are initially asked to learn begin with consonant sounds.

3. Although initial emphasis is placed on consonants, there is an early (readiness, preprimer, and primer texts) introduction of some vowels that allows children to decode meaningful words from the very early stages of reading instruction and provides them with skills that allow some degree of independence.

4. Practically all phonics content is taught by the end of second grade. In most basal series only a few of the most difficult or infrequent letter–sound combinations are taught as late as third grade.

5. Most basal reading series include word patterns or *phonograms* at the start of their reading programs.

As shown by the above observations, not all consonant sounds are taught before vowels are introduced. Remember that some consonants rarely occur in words and need not be addressed in beginning reading. In addition, every word has at least one vowel letter.

CONSONANTS

At this point, a review of the consonant phonemes is in order. As discussed in Chapter 5, there are 25 consonant phonemes, 18 of which are composed of single letters and 7 of which are composed of two-letter combinations. Fill in a key word that contains the sound of each two-letter phoneme.

/b/	bat	/ch/	_____
/d/	did	/hw/	_____
/f/	fat	/ng/	_____
/g/	go	/sh/	_____
/h/	he	/th/	_____
/j/	jam	/TH/	_____
/k/	kid	/zh/	_____
/l/	let		
/m/	me		
/m/	no		
/p/	pan		
/r/	run		
/s/	sat		
/t/	ten		
/v/	very		
/w/	will		
/y/	yes		
/z/	zoo		

Up to this point in the text, an instructional emphasis has been placed on learning phonemes. In teaching phonics, however, one begins with letters or graphemes and teaches children to recognize the sounds that correspond to them. The difficulty of this task is proportionately related to the level of consistency existing between letters and sounds. Because consonants are far more consistent in their spelling/sound relationships than are vowels, they are less confusing to children. Still, various problems arise when teaching consonants.

Single Consonants

Of the 21 consonant letters, 17 are basically phonemically consistent when they occur by themselves and not in combination (digraphs) with other letters. These include the following:

b   d   f   h   j   k   l   m   n   p   q   r   t   v   w   y   z

The four consonant letters that do not show a somewhat consistent one-to-one correspondence between letter and phoneme are *c, g, s,* and *x.* Each will be discussed separately below.

The letter C: C generally represents two phonemes, /k/ and /s/. (Remember, the letter *c* does not represent a phoneme identified by its own name.)

city	/s/	pact	/k/
coat	/k/	receive	/s/
rice	/s/	action	/k/

When the letter *c* represents /s/, it is commonly called the "soft c." When it represents /k/, it is commonly called the "hard c." Generally, the "hard c" is taught first because it occurs more frequently, especially as an initial letter in words.

The letter G: G generally represents two phonemes, /g/ and /j/.

go	/g/	gull	/g/
gym	/j/	wage	/j/
agile	/j/	nag	/g/

When *g* represents /j/, it is commonly called the "soft g." When it represents /g/, it is commonly called the "hard g." Generally, the "hard g" is taught first for the same reasons that "hard c" is taught first.

The letter S: S generally represents two phonemes, /s/ and /z/, with /s/ being taught first.

smile	/s/	his	/z/
season	/z/	tops	/s/
is	/z/	test	/s/

The letter X: X generally represents three phonemes: /z/; /k/ /s/; /g/ /z/. (Remember that *x* does not represent a phoneme that is identified by its own name.)

sox	/k/ /s/		expect	/k/ /s/
exit	/g/ /z/ or /k/ /s/		mix	/k/ /s/
anxiety	/g/ /z/		xerox	/z/

Although the most common single letter–sound relationships have been discussed above and should be adequate for phonics instruction, there are many exceptions to these. Fortunately, they occur infrequently. Here is a sampling of some of these exceptions:

of   /v/

individual	/j/
pleasure	/zh/
sure	/sh/
cello	/ch/
think	/ng/

Consonant Blends (Clusters)

Consonant blends are sounds in a syllable represented by two or more letters that are blended together *without* losing their own identity. Although blends are actually separate sounds, they are dealt with together because they occur frequently in syllables.

Initial consonant blends frequently taught in current basal series include the following:

br	fr	tr	fl	sc	sn	sw
cr	gr	bl	gl	sl	sp	spr
dr	pr	cl	pl	sm	st	str

Final consonant blends frequently taught in current basal series include the following:

-ld (cold)	-lk (walk)	-nd (pond)	-nk (drink)	-nt (want)
-mp (lamp)	-sk (ask)	-st (last)	-ft (lift)	-lt (colt)

Consonant Digraphs

To review, consonant digraphs consist of two letters that stand for a single phoneme. Several letter combinations are classified as consonant digraphs. In teaching phonics, however, a limited number of these digraphs must be taught. Children should learn that either some letter combinations represent a new sound that is different from the sound represented by each letter separately, or one of the two letters is silent. Although basals vary in the consonant digraphs they teach, the following occur most frequently:

Initial Consonant Digraphs
ch (chubby)	ph (phone)	wh (why)
gn (gnat)	sh (she)	wr (wrong)
kn (known)	th (the)	

Ending Consonant Digraphs
-ch (lunch)	-gh (tough)	-ng (sing)
-ck (luck)	-ll (call)	-ss (class)
-ff (off)	-mb (lamb)	-th (teeth)

Of these consonant digraphs, *th* and *ch* create the most confusion because they are inconsistent and frequently represent more than one sound.

The consonant digraph Th: *Th* can represent one of two phonemes, /th/ or /TH/. One is called a voiceless sound (/th/) because when spoken, air is expelled and little vibration is created by the voice box or tongue. Try the following voiceless /th/ sounds.

thing	thigh	thank	thumb
bath	ether	cloth	teeth

The other sound associated with the consonant digraph *th* is called a voiced sound (/TH/) because when spoken, little air is expelled and a definite vibration is created in the voice box and by the tongue. Try the following voiced /TH/ sounds.

then	clothe	this	these
thy	their	bathe	either

When teaching the sounds associated with *th,* it is not necessary to burden children with the terms *voiceless* and *voiced.* Simply pointing out to children the fact that *th* can represent one of two sounds as heard in designated key words will suffice.

The consonant digraph Ch: *Ch* usually represents the phoneme /ch/, as in *church.* Less frequently, *ch* represents the phoneme /k/, as in *chemical,* and the phoneme /sh/, as in *machine.*

VOWELS

Due to the inconsistent nature of the sounds that vowel letters represent, teaching vowel sounds is the most difficult task in phonics instruction. Because of this inconsistency, one must be careful to avoid any vowel instruction that will confuse rather than assist children in attacking unknown words. An examination of the phonics content of current basal series leads to several observations:

1. The scope and sequence of vowel instruction varies widely. Research has not identified the best sequence in which vowels should be taught.
2. Although formal instruction places initial emphasis on consonant sounds, vowels are introduced early. Vowel instruction is begun at either the readiness and preprimer text levels or the primer text level.
3. The greater part of vowel instruction up to first grade is devoted to short vowel sounds and long vowel sounds as represented by certain vowel digraphs (*ai, ay, ea, ee*) or words having the spelling pattern, vowel-consonant-*e* (i.e., *hope, take*).

4. Increased attention is being given to teaching vowel sounds within particular rimes as represented by phonograms. This approach takes advantage of the fact that vowel sounds are far more stable within particular rimes than they are in isolation.

5. The schwa sound is often introduced at approximately the second- or third-grade level. It is generally taught as the initial sound of a two-syllable word beginning with the letter *a*, such as *about*.

6. Instruction in some of the most difficult vowel digraphs and diphthongs is delayed until third grade.

A review of the 19 vowel phonemes follows:

/ā/	age	/ē/	ease	/ī/	ice	/ō/	old	/ū/	use
/ă/	an	/ĕ/	end	/ĭ/	in	/ŏ/	odd	/ŭ/	up
/oi/	oil (diphthong)			/ou/	out (diphthong)		
/ōō/	too			/ŏŏ/	good		/ə/	about
/â/	dare	/û/	her	/ä/	father		/ô/	off

As mentioned earlier in this chapter, when teaching phonics, one begins with letters or graphemes and teaches children to recognize the sounds that correspond to them. Because vowels are not consistent in their spellings, this becomes a formidable task.

Short–Long Vowel Sounds

Short vowel sounds are usually introduced in three-letter words with a spelling pattern of consonant-vowel-consonant (CVC). This is expanded to include words that follow the spelling patterns VC and CVCC. Several techniques can be used for formal instruction of short vowels. Two examples are:

1. Using phonograms to build word families. For instance, using the phonogram *ig*, one could develop the following word family: big, dig, pig, fig, wig.

2. Changing the vowel sound in known words to make new words: big, bag; dig, dog; wig, wag.

In contrast to short vowels, long vowels are usually introduced in words with a spelling pattern of VCe, as in *whale*. This is expanded to include certain vowel digraphs (*oa* in *boat*), and single-syllable words ending in a vowel (*o* as in *go*).

Children are often taught or led to discover generalizations that will assist them in identifying short and long vowel sounds. The following examples are from current basal series and illustrate varied approaches.

Silver Burdett Ginn, 1993: "Say these words, elongating the vowel sound as you say each one: *man, pet, pin, nod, tub.* Point out that these words all have short vowel sounds. Say these words: *mane, Pete, pine, rode, tube.* Explain that these words all have long vowel sounds. Write each set of words on the chalkboard and have children compare both sets. Lead them to see that short vowel words have a consonant-vowel-consonant pattern and long vowel words have a consonant-vowel-consonant-*e* pattern" (Silver Burdett Ginn, 1993, p. T71).

Houghton Mifflin, 1997c: "Have children read the first two sentences on page 10 with you. Ask them to listen for the vowel sounds in *no* and *mop.* Write the words on the chalkboard. Ask these questions:

> What vowel sound do you hear in *mop?* (short o)
>
> Do you hear the same vowel sound in *no?* (no)

Remind children that the vowel sound in *no* is the long *o* sound. Label the CV pattern in *no.* You may also want to have children contrast these words: not–no; got–go" (Houghton, Mifflin, 1997c, p. T69).

Vowel Digraphs

Vowel digraphs are two-vowel letters that stand for a single sound or phoneme. Several letter combinations are classified as vowel digraphs. In teaching phonics, however, only a limited number of these digraphs must be taught because many vowel digraphs are not consistent enough in their spelling/sound relationships to justify teaching them.

An analysis of current basal series reveals that most include instruction for the following vowel digraphs:

Vowel Digraphs	*Phonemes*
ee, ea	/ē/
ai, ay	/ā/
oa, ow	/ō/
oo	/o͞o/
oo	/o͝o/
ou, ow	/ou/ (diphthong)
oi, oy	/oi/ (diphthong)
au, aw	/ô/

In teaching vowel digraphs, basals tend to emphasize the most common sound represented by specific digraph combinations. These basals also point out that some vowel digraphs (*oi, oy, ou, ow, oo*) are special cases and represent sounds that are neither long nor short.

R-Controlled Vowels

Children are taught that when a vowel is followed by the consonant letter *r*, the vowel sound is neither short nor long:

> Read aloud the sentence on page 18 and point out the word *shark*. Explain that when a vowel is followed by an *r*, the vowel sound is neither long nor short, and that the letters *ar* often stand for the vowel sound heard in *shark*.
>
> Ask children to look on page 19 and find three other words in which *ar* stands for the sound heard in *shark* (are, far, apart).
>
> Next, explain that the sound for *o* followed by *r* is neither long nor short. Ask a volunteer to read page 20. Point to *for* and explain that the letters *or* often stand for the vowel sound in *for* (Houghton Mifflin, 1997a, p. T257).

Schwa

The schwa sound is introduced at approximately the second- or third-grade level and is often taught in conjunction with syllabication and/or dictionary use. Although the schwa represents the sound for which many different letters stand, little attention is given to the teaching of the schwa sound.

A schwa is a short, unstressed vowel that often occurs in unaccented syllables. Therefore, children would have to divide words into proper syllables, identify which syllables are unaccented, and finally, determine which vowels were schwas. Obviously, this systematic approach is beyond the capabilities of young children. Little instructional attention, therefore, is given to teaching children how to decode the schwa sound in a technical, systematic manner. Fortunately, since the schwa sound is a soft vowel sound that is similar to the short *u* sound, children often come close enough to the sound to render a correct pronunciation in their decoding attempts.

Teaching Vowels Through Phonograms

Wiley & Durrell (1970) conducted a study showing that the following 37 phonograms can be combined with various consonant letters to generate approximately 500 primary words:

-ack	-ail	-ain	-ake	-ale	-ame	-an
-ank	-ap	-ash	-at	-ate	-aw	-ay
-eat	-ell	-est	-ice	-ick	-ide	-ight
-ill	-in	-ine	-ing	-ink	-ip	-it
-ock	-oke	-op	-ore	-ot	-uck	-ug
-ump	-unk					

Wiley & Durrell (1970) found that children learned the vowel sounds contained in phonograms more easily compared to learning these sounds through individual letter–sound correspondences or phonic generalizations.

■ ■ ■   **CHAPTER 7: PRACTICE**

1. The inconsistent spelling of (consonant sounds, vowel sounds) is a basic problem of phonics. (Circle one.)

2. There are _____ vowel phonemes in the English language.

3. There (is, is not) a best sequence in which vowels should be taught. (Circle one.)

4. Of the 21 single consonant letters, four are phonemically inconsistent and represent more than one sound. Alphabetically list the four consonant letters, indicate the phonemes they can represent, and write out a key word for each.

Letter	Phonemes	Words
_____	/__/, /__/	_____, _____
_____	/__/, /__/	_____, _____
_____	/__/, /__/	_____, _____
_____	/__/	_____
	/__/ /__/	_____
	/__/ /__/	_____

5. The "soft c" is represented by the phoneme /__/.
   The "hard c" is represented by the phoneme /__/.
   The "soft g" is represented by the phoneme /__/.
   The "hard g" is represented by the phoneme /__/.

6. (Consonant digraphs, Consonant blends) are sounds in a syllable represented by two or more letters that are combined without losing their individual identity. (Circle one.)

7. Can you discriminate between consonant digraphs and consonant blends? Write "D" after letter combinations that represent digraphs and "B" after letter combinations that represent blends.

br _____	pl _____	-ck _____	-sk _____
ch _____	sh _____	-nk _____	-ld _____
cl _____	wh _____	-mp _____	-ng _____
kn _____	pr _____	-mb _____	-st _____
th _____	gr _____	-nt _____	-nd _____

8. What is the advantage of teaching vowel sounds within phonograms as compared to teaching them in isolation?

_____

_____

_____

_____

_____

_____

_____

9. Develop and write out two instructional activities that will teach children to recognize the appropriate sounds of vowel digraphs.

a. _____

_____

_____

_____

_____

b. _____

_____

_____

_____

_____

10. Develop and write out two instructional activities that will teach children to recognize the appropriate sounds of r-controlled vowels.

a. _____

_____

_____

_____

_____

b. _____

_____

_____

_____

_____

_____

11. Develop and write out two instructional activities/games that use phonograms to assist children in learning to recognize vowel sounds.

a. _____

_____

_____

_____

_____

_____

b. _____

_____

_____

_____

_____

_____

■ ■ ■ **CUMULATIVE REVIEW OF CHAPTERS 1 THROUGH 7**

1. Phonics (appears, does not appear) to be the panacea for most reading ills. (Circle one.)
2. Phonics instruction should be completed by the end of _____ grade for most children.
3. Define the following terms:

Phonics: _____

_____

_____

Phoneme: _____

_____

_____

Open syllable: _____

_____

_____

Macron: _____

_____

Consonant: _____

Digraph: _____

Syllable: _____

4. The authors of *Becoming a Nation of Readers* recommend that reading readiness programs focus on _____, _____, and oral language.

5. Underline any consonant or vowel digraph contained in the following words.

   out   book   blunt   stun   that
   dare   song   chat   knob   clip

6. A _____ of two letters is called a digraph.

7. What is emergent literacy and how does it affect learning to read once children enter school?

   _____
   _____
   _____
   _____
   _____
   _____

8. How might teachers use the *Mental Measurement Yearbooks* to their advantage?

   _____
   _____
   _____

9. Studies have shown that children who begin their schooling knowing the ABCs are more likely to become better readers than children who

lack this knowledge. Of what importance is this fact for teachers of beginning reading?

_____

_____

_____

_____

_____

_____

_____

_____

10. Fill in the proper consonant phoneme for each of the underlined letter(s).

cage	/__/	queen	/__/ /__/
who	/__/	sox	/__/ /__/
knew	/__/	cell	/__/
measure	/__/	critique	/__/

11. Fill in the proper vowel phoneme for each of the underlined letter(s).

air	/__/	toe	/__/
senator	/__/	call	/__/
otter	/__/	house	/__/
turn	/__/	good	/__/

12. How many phonemes are represented in the following words? Write each word using its phoneme pronunciation symbols.

red	_____	_____
coat	_____	_____
wheel	_____	_____
quit	_____	_____
who	_____	_____
when	_____	_____
fly	_____	_____
curse	_____	_____
dialect	_____	_____

13. Write out the vowel generalization that the words below follow:
coat

_____

_____

hope

_____

_____

she

_____

_____

but

_____

_____

14. Why is it more effective to teach vowel _generalizations_ rather than vowel _rules_?

_____

_____

_____

_____

_____

_____

_____

_____

_____

_____

8

■ ■ ■ ■ ■

Syllabication/Accenting

At first glance, especially for those who are competent readers, the process of syllabication appears to be a somewhat simple task. On closer examination, however, it reveals itself to be a rather complex process that many children find quite difficult. Why, then, should the process be taught to children? The answer lies in the fact that unless some systematic procedure is used when attempting to decode multisyllabic words, the process essentially becomes one of trial and error. By providing children with strategies for syllabication, the amount of trial and error needed to decode unknown words is reduced significantly. Even though a certain amount of trial and error will remain, it becomes less random and more directed.

A syllable is a unit of pronunciation consisting of a vowel alone or a vowel with one or more consonants. There is only one vowel phoneme in each syllable. Phonic generalizations pertain to syllables, not to words, which means that syllables, not words, are initially decoded. For this reason, the vowel generalizations presented in Chapter 6 were stated in terms of syllables.

As children begin to work with an increasing number of unknown polysyllabic words, they must be able to syllabicate them correctly first before applying vowel generalizations. Since they cannot divide unknown words by sound, they must rely on certain spelling patterns and/or generalizations to assist them in this task.

Before attempting to teach children syllabication strategies or generalizations, the prerequisite skills of hearing and recognizing syllables in words, understanding letter–sound relationships, and knowing the useful phonic generalizations must be learned. It is not unusual, then, for the topic of syllabication to be introduced as late as the second or third grade.

Children are commonly introduced to the topic of syllabication through the process of getting them to hear syllables in words they already know. The activity of clapping each syllable as they say words is often used at this introductory stage of instruction. Although it is appropriate to have children practice syllabication with known words at the onset of instruction when the concept is introduced, it is inappropriate to have children practice their syllabication skills on known words. To be effective, reinforcement and practice must be done using unknown words. Therefore, the practice items offered in this chapter consist mostly of nonsense words. These will encourage the mature readers of this text to experience and use the strategies and generalizations that their future students will need to use when they attempt to decode unknown multisyllabic words. Syllabication generalizations that should assist children in their attempts to decode multisyllabic words include the following.

1. Every syllable contains one, and only one, vowel sound. As mentioned above, this concept is best developed by assisting children to recognize syllables in words they already know. This task is accomplished through providing children with varied opportunities to hear and recognize syllables in spoken words. Eventually children should be able to pronounce familiar words in syllabic form. Once children understand the concept of syllabication and know letter–sound relationships and appropriate phonic generalizations, attention is turned to an analysis of word structure and the spelling patterns of words.

2. Most affixes (prefixes and suffixes) are syllables. Children are taught to look first for common word parts (prefixes and suffixes) that they have learned previously. Some of the most common prefixes and suffixes follow:

Prefix

dis-	in-	non-	sub-
em-	inter-	over-	un-
en-	ir-	pre-	
im-	mis-	re-	

Suffix

-able	-est	-ly	-y
-al	-ful	-ment	
-en	-ing	-ness	
-er	-less	-ion (-tion)	

Often, more specific generalizations related to affixes are taught as follows:

    a. *-ture* and *-tion* are syllables (e.g., pic-ture, ma-ture, cap-tion, lo-tion).

b. The inflected -*ed* adds a syllable when affixed to a verb ending in -*d* or -*t*. Otherwise, it does not add a syllable (e.g., need-ed, root-ed, stayed, asked.)

3. In a compound word, the syllabic division usually comes between the words of which it is composed. Syllabicate divided compound words according to other generalizations.

4. When a word ends in -*le* preceded by a consonant, the consonant plus -*le* comprise a syllable (e.g., mid-dle, ar-ti-cle).

5. When two vowel letters appear together, they usually represent one sound and should be viewed as a single grapheme when syllabicating. Burmeister (1966) examined the validity of this generalization using randomly selected words from the *Teacher's Word Book of 30,000 Words* (Thorndike & Lorge, 1944) and found that 84.5 percent of the time it proved true. In addition, one-third of the exceptions occurred when the vowel pair *ia* appeared in words such as *giant*.

6. Letters representing consonant digraphs, especially *th, ch,* and *sh,* and consonant blends are treated as single consonants and are not separated when words are broken into syllables.

7. Although double consonant letters are generally separated when words are broken into syllables via writing, the sound will be represented in only one syllable as follows:

common	com-mon	kŏm-ən
latter	lat-ter	lăt-ər
connote	con-note	kə-nōt

Once these specific generalizations above are addressed, the following generalizations are applied.

8. When two consonants are between two vowels, a syllabic division often occurs between the consonants. A current basal series expresses this generalization as follows: "Most VCCV words are divided into syllables between the consonants" (Houghton Mifflin, 1997b, p. 323E).

9. When there is one consonant between two vowels, the consonant often goes with the next syllable. This generalization has less consistency than does number 8 above (see Table 1, pp. 50–53, numbers 38 and 39). For this reason, basals usually present options as follows: "Most VCV words with the short-vowel pattern in the first syllable are divided after the consonant because the consonant is part of the short-vowel pattern. Most VCV words with a long-vowel sound or a *schwa* sound in the first syllable are divided before the consonant" (Houghton Mifflin, 1997b, p. 323E). Thus, students are told when they attempt to figure out an unfamiliar word syllable by syllable, they "might have to

make several attempts, trying different pronunciations and stressing different syllables, before coming up with a word that sounds familiar" (Houghton Mifflin, 1997b, p. 323E).

In terms of accenting, two generalizations should suffice.

1. In two-syllable words, the accent is usually on the first syllable.
2. Prefixes and suffixes are generally not accented.

As you teach children generalizations that apply to syllabication and accenting, it is important to teach the concept that these provide a starting point in their attempts to decode words. If their efforts yield words that do not make sense or are unknown, alternative efforts should be attempted. Teachers should no longer attempt to teach these generalizations as though they were *rules* that produce results without failure.

■ ■ ■   **CHAPTER 8: PRACTICE**

1. In a two-syllable word, the accent is usually on the _____ syllable.
2. Every syllable contains one, and only one, _____ sound.
3. Most affixes (are, are not) syllables. (Circle one.)
4. The inflected -*ed* adds a syllable when affixed to a verb that ends with either the letter _____ or _____.
5. In writing, double consonants are usually broken up into separate syllables. In speech, how is the pronunciation of double consonants handled?

_____

_____

_____

_____

_____

6. Letters representing consonant digraphs, especially *th, ch,* and *sh,* and consonant blends are treated as single consonants and (are, are not) separated when words are broken into syllables. (Circle one.)
7. When two vowel letters appear together, they usually represent _____ sound.
8. Indicate where the syllabic divisions occur in the following vowel-consonant patterns, nonsense words, or words. There are no consonant digraphs in the first four letter patterns. In the space provided, indicate which generalization(s) you used to accomplish this task.

Vowel-Consonant Letter Patterns

a. VCVC _____
b. CVCCV _____
c. CCVCCVC _____
d. CCVCVC _____

Real Words

e. amass _____
f. aphis _____
g. beldam _____
h. bolide _____
i. cupule _____
j. dispensary _____
k. furbelow _____
l. judicature _____

Nonsense Words

m. preanthema _____
n. unboted _____
o. emakle _____
p. epeture _____
q. grapeet _____
r. resired _____
s. ecad _____
t. antole _____
u. scrnt _____
v. mashot _____
w. haulm _____
x. subtonen _____
y. latton _____

■ ■ ■ **CUMULATIVE REVIEW OF CHAPTERS 1 THROUGH 8**

1. Workbooks and other paper-and-pencil activities require students to learn or practice phonics silently. Is this an effective approach? Why?

_____
_____
_____
_____
_____

2. Define the following terms:

Phonetics: _____

Grapheme: _____

Vowels: _____

Diphthong: _____

Consonant blend: _____

Rime: _____

Schwa: _____

3. When a cumulative file contains information indicating a child has successfully passed a vision test, why might this information be misleading?

_____

_____

_____

_____

4. What relationship appears to exist between oral language and reading achievement?

_____

_____

_____

_____

_____

_____

_____

_____

5. What is the difference between phoneme segmentation and phoneme blending? Provide an example of each approach.

_____

_____

_____

_____

_____

_____

_____

_____

6. Fill in the proper vowel or consonant phoneme for each underlined letter(s).

plaid	/__/	pleasure	/__/
mare	/__/	long	/__/
sky	/__/	basic	/__/
toy	/__/	ghost	/__/

7. What instructional implications does Clymer's 1963 study hold for the teaching of phonic generalizations?

_____

_____

_____

_____

8. What is the difference between an inductive approach to teaching phonics and a deductive approach? Is one better than the other? Explain.

_____

_____

_____

_____

_____

9. Formal instruction in phonics usually begins with an emphasis on in-tial _____ sounds. Why?

_____

_____

_____

_____

_____

10. Identify a phonogram and indicate how to develop a word family instructionally.

_____

_____

_____

_____

_____

_____

_____

11. How does the ability to syllabicate words assist children in their attempts to pronounce unknown words?

_____

_____

_____

_____

_____

_____

_____

9

■ ■ ■ ■ ■

Diagnostic Teaching

The goal of every teacher should be to provide an environment in which children are allowed the opportunity to grow toward their full potential. This learning environment can be accomplished only if teachers are able to identify the individual strengths and weaknesses of students, and can develop instructional strategies that take advantage of this knowledge. In essence, it requires every classroom teacher to participate in diagnostic teaching.

To assume this diagnostic role effectively, teachers need to become aware of the general principles of diagnosis as well as the elements of diagnosis related to specific content areas. Discussion of both the general principles of diagnosis and specific procedures for diagnosing phonics follow.

GENERAL PRINCIPLES OF DIAGNOSIS

General diagnostic principles include the following:

1. Diagnosis should be viewed as a daily occurrence. Diagnosis is too often treated as a special event that takes place only once or twice a year. In reality, teachers need to observe and evaluate children on a continuing basis because children's needs and/or skills can change drastically over a short period.

2. Decisions about children should be based on diagnostic information collected from various sources. Instructional decisions about children should never be made based on a single test or observation. Generally, the more diverse the data that teachers collect, the more useful is the information.

3. The identification of patterns of errors should be emphasized when analyzing diagnostic information. If a type of error occurs in a pattern, greater confidence can be placed on the interpretation that the error is

truly a problem for the child. When decisions are based on isolated errors, unneeded instruction and practice often follow.

4. Work on only one or two reading weaknesses at a time. Often, when diagnosing children who exhibit problems in reading, several weaknesses will be identified. If attempts are made to remediate all of these weaknesses at once, it generally overwhelms the children and further frustrates their efforts to improve. Narrow the skills to be taught to the one or two that appear to create the most difficulty and remediate these before continuing with others that are less debilitating.

5. Diagnosis for its own sake is not acceptable; it must lead to specific instructional action. Teachers must avoid becoming so enamored of the diagnostic process that they lose sight of the ultimate objective of diagnosis—the identification and remediation of weaknesses or disabilities.

The procedures for evaluating phonic skills are varied and include both informal and formal diagnosis. The following is a sample of procedures teachers can use and items they can construct to assist them in diagnosing students' phonic skills.

PROCEDURES FOR DIAGNOSING PHONIC SKILLS

Observation

During a typical school day, teachers have many opportunities to observe and collect pertinent information about the reading proficiencies of students. To take advantage of these opportunities, teachers need to devise written systems that allow them to record their observations over time. These, in turn, can be analyzed later to identify weaknesses or patterns of error. These observations can also be used to verify or question results gathered through more formalized data collections.

There is no best way to collect and categorize observational data. This process can be as simple as developing a file for each child and recording observations by date as they occur, similar to the system used by medical doctors. Or more specific observational documents can be constructed by teachers to identify the exact phonic skills to be observed. For example, if one of the skills a teacher decides to analyze is the ability to pronounce initial consonants correctly in single-syllable words, the teacher can simply construct a sheet with the consonant letters listed on it and mark them off as children pronounce each consonant. Teachers can observe and/or develop recording sheets related to phonic elements such as single-letter consonant sounds, double-letter consonant sounds, consonant blends, long vowels, short vowels, r-controlled vowels, diphthongs, vowel combinations (especially *ee, ea, ai, ay, oa*), double *o*, knowledge of vowel and consonant generalizations, phoneme segmentation, and phoneme blending.

Informal Reading Inventory (IRI)

The IRI is a more formal procedure for observing, recording, and analyzing children's reading proficiencies. Generally, these inventories attempt to measure, through the oral reading of a set of graded word lists and paragraphs, both the word recognition and comprehension skills of those taking the test. As the examinee reads the word lists and paragraphs for the word recognition part of the inventory, all errors are recorded on a sheet that is later used to analyze and categorize the types of errors that the examinee made (similar to the teacher's written comments mentioned under the previous heading "Observation").

The IRI has certain limitations that teachers should recognize. It can be administered to only one person at a time and requires a significant amount of time to administer and analyze. For these reasons, many reading authorities feel that it is impractical to recommend that the IRI be administered to every child in a class. Rather, it might best be administered to those who are having significant problems in reading and about whom teachers feel they need more information. Another limitation that must be recognized is the fact that data from an IRI are but one sample of behavior that has been gathered at a specific point in time. The data may or may not be representative of the child's real skills. Therefore, even if an IRI is given, the data should be tested by comparing the results to data gathered through teacher observations and other evaluative procedures.

Several standardized tests fall under the category of informal reading inventories. Some that are common in the field include:

> *Classroom Reading Inventory,* Seventh Edition, by Nicholas J. Silvaroli. (1994). Brown & Benchmark: Dubuque, IA.
>
> *Ekwall Reading Inventory,* Second Edition, by Eldon E. Ekwall. (1986). Allyn and Bacon: Newton, MA.
>
> *Basic Reading Inventory,* Fifth Edition, by Jerry L. Johns. (1991). Kendall/Hunt: Dubuque, IA.

For an evaluation of these instruments, consult the latest *Mental Measurement Yearbook* (the twelfth yearbook is the most recent).

Phonemic Awareness

A high correlation exists between the ability to recognize spoken words as a sequence of individual sounds and reading achievement. We have seen that explicit instruction can increase the phonemic awareness of children. To assist in determining the level of phonemic awareness in children, the following assessment items can be used.

Assessment 1: Isolation of beginning sounds. Ask the child what the first sounds of selected words are.

"What is the first sound of *dog*?"

Assessment 2: Deletion of initial sound. Read a word and ask the child to say it without the first sound.

"Say the word *cat*. Say *cat* without the /k/."

To begin, it is probably better to use words that will remain words when the first letter is eliminated.

Assessment 3: Segmentation of phonemes. Ask the child to say aloud the separate sounds of a word that is read.

"What are the two sounds in the word *go*?"

Assessment 4: Blending of phonemes. Slowly read the individual sounds of a word and ask the child to say what the word is.

"What word am I saying? /d/ /ô/ /g/."

Assessment 5: Phoneme manipulation. Read a word and ask the child to replace the initial sound with another. Have the child say the new word.

"In the word *fan*, the first sound is a /f/. If you replace the /f/ with an /m/, how would you say the new word?"

Letter Names

As discussed earlier in the readiness chapter (Chapter 4), knowledge of letter names is not a prerequisite for learning to read. Although knowledge of letter names on entering school appears to be a predictor of later reading success, the relationship between knowing letter names and reading achievement is not one of cause and effect. Based on a review of the research related to this issue, however, Groff (1984) states:

> At present, the following conclusion seems tenable: Letter name teaching is appropriate if done concurrently with instruction in phonics. Those who contend that the time of letter name teaching is unimportant probably are wrong.
>
> Since letter name knowledge and phonics knowledge are highly correlated, it makes sense to view them as functionally related areas of information. Thus, simultaneous teaching appears to be the best way to exploit their potential for helping children to learn to read (p. 387).

Thus, it seems desirable at the beginning stages of reading instruction to assess children's knowledge of letter names. This information can be gleaned through assessments similar to those listed below.

Assessment 1:   Develop flash cards for each letter of the alphabet, starting with lowercase. (Once lowercase letters are known, this exercise can be expanded to include uppercase letters.) In random order, present each card to the examinee and ask the student to name the letter. Record the examinee's responses on a scoring sheet. This data can be used to determine the appropriate letter name instruction for each child.

Assessment 2:   Have the examinee write the letters of the alphabet as they are dictated in a random order. Analyze the results to determine which letters the examinee knows. Since the goal is letter name knowledge, either lower- or uppercase responses are correct. Responses that show the reverse (i.e., mirror image) form of a letter should also be considered correct.

Consonant Sounds

Several types of items can be used to determine if children understand the relationship between consonants and the letters that represent them. Most of the following examples offer ways of measuring recognition of the initial letter or letters of words (a) because of the essential role that this position plays in decoding words and (b) because this is the position that is addressed first in instruction. However, the same kinds of assessments can be constructed for the endings of words as well.

Assessment 1:   Letter to sound—single-consonant letters. Using flash cards of 19 single consonant letters (q and x do not have to be addressed at the beginning level), ask the child to say the sound represented by each. Record the child's responses.

Assessment 2:   Letter to sound—single-consonant letters/pictures. Show the child a consonant letter followed by three pictures that name something. Ask the child to identify the picture whose name begins with the same sound as represented by the consonant letter. As examiner, name each picture slowly. Record the child's responses. The same 19 single-consonant letters as indicated in Assessment 1 above should be evaluated.

      m   [pictures of a]   (ball)   (moon)   (toy)

Assessment 3:   Sound to letter—single-consonant letters. Provide the child with a score sheet that has four consonant letters after each item. For each, say a word and tell the child to circle the consonant letter that represents the first sound of the word.

      toy   s   t   m   p

Assessment 4:   Sound to letter—single-consonant letters. Have the child write the beginning letter of each word that you read. Vary words to include all 19 consonant letters mentioned in Assessment 1 above.

Assessment 5:   Letter to sound—consonant digraphs. Using flash cards of consonant digraphs (*th, ch, sh, wh*), ask the child to say the sound represented by each letter pair. Record the child's responses.

Assessment 6:   Letter to sound—consonant digraphs/pictures. Show the child a consonant digraph followed by three pictures that name something. Ask the child to identify the picture whose name begins with the same sound as represented by the two letters. As examiner, name each picture slowly. Record the child's responses. The same four consonant digraphs as indicated in Assessment 3 above should be evaluated.

    sh   [pictures of a]   (ship)   (church)   (sun)

Assessment 7:   Sound to letters—consonant digraphs. Provide the child with a score sheet that has four consonant digraphs after each item. For each, say a word and tell the child to circle the consonant digraph that represents the first sound of the word.

    chin   sh   th   ch   wh

Assessment 8:   Sound to letters—consonant digraphs. Have the child write the first two letters of each word that you read. Vary the words so that they begin with *sh, th, ch,* and *wh.*

Assessment 9:   Consonant letters representing blends. Using flash cards of letters representing several blends, ask the child to say the sound represented by each. Record the child's responses.

Assessment 10:   Consonant letters representing blends/pictures. Show the child letters representing consonant blends followed by three pictures that name something. Ask the child to identify the picture whose name begins with the same sounds as represented by the consonant letters. As examiner, name each picture slowly. Record the child's responses.

    tr   [pictures of a]   (top)   (train)   (thumb)

Assessment 11:   Consonant letters representing blends—sound to letters. Provide the child with a score sheet that has letters representing four consonant blends after each item. For each, say a word and tell the child to circle the letters that represent the first sounds of the word.

    blue   bl   st   br   fl

Assessment 12:   Consonant letters representing blends—sound to letters. Have the child write the first two letters of each word that you read. Vary the words to include several beginning blends.

Assessment 13:   Consonant letters representing blends—phonograms. Construct words combining common phonograms (i.e., *an, ill, ig*) with letters representing blends. After reading and emphasizing the rime (the sound of a phonogram) part of the word family, ask the child to read the words of the family. Record the child's responses. Children may need the examiner to model this behavior for a couple of families.

an   bran   stan   blan   clan

Vowel Sounds

The following assessments measure children's knowledge about vowels.

Assessment 1:   Long and short vowels. Display flash cards of the 5 vowel letters (*a, e, i, o, u*) and ask the child to identify verbally the long sound and the short sound of each. Record the child's responses.

Assessment 2:   Short vowels. Read sets of three words, each containing the same medial vowel sound (short), and have the examinee write or verbally indicate what vowel sound the words contain. Vary sets to include all short vowel sounds.

pin   bit   him

Assessment 3:   Short vowels. Develop sets of 5 words (some will be nonsense words*) that vary only by a medial vowel. Have the child read each word list. Record the child's responses.

mat	pan	sap
met	pen	sep
mit	pin	sip
mot	pon	sop
mut	pun	sup

Assessment 4:   Long vowels. Read sets of three words, each containing the same medial vowel sound (long), and have the examinee write or indicate verbally what vowel sound the words contain. Vary sets to include all long vowel sounds.

site   night   live

Assessment 5:   Long vowels (vowel–consonant–final *e* pattern). Develop sets of 5 words following the VCe pattern (some will be nonsense words), each with a different initial vowel letter. Have the child read each word list. Record the child's responses.

---

*When evaluating phonic skills with items that require the examinee to go from graphs to sounds, it is important to use words that are not part of the child's sight vocabulary. Therefore, this assessment and several that follow include nonsense words as a guard against obtaining misleading information.

cake	pete	sime	rote	mute
gate	scene	mite	home	fuse
sate	pese	like	hoke	cube

Assessment 6:   Short vowels (CVC) and long vowels (CVe). Develop a list of real-word and nonsense-word pairs that vary by a final *e*. Have the child read the word list and ask why she pronounced the words that way. Record the child's responses.

rote	rot
mit	mite
make	mak
set	sete
tune	tun

Assessment 7:   Vowel digraphs. Develop a list of real words and nonsense words that contain the vowel digraphs (*ee, ea, ai, ay, oa*). Have the child read the word list. Record the child's responses.

keep	say
teap	mait
seat	seet
tay	boat
pain	soan

Assessment 8:   Special digraphs. Develop a list of real words and non-sense words that contain special vowel digraphs (*oi, oy, ou, ow, oo, au*). Have the child read the word list. Record the child's responses.

soil	mou
koo	boy
out	poit
poy	cow
too	sook
dow	maul
good	paut

Assessment 9:   r-controlled vowels. Develop a list of real words and non-sense words that contain r-controlled vowels. Have the child read the word list. Record the child's responses.

car	sert

purm	dare
turn	lar
sare	firm
term	kirn

CONCLUSION

It is not the intention of this chapter to suggest that teachers should construct instruments that contain all of the assessment items discussed in the chapter. The teacher is in the best position to determine what diagnostic information may be needed. Therefore, the representative assessment items included in the text should be considered as resource data from which teachers can pick and choose to assist in developing their own teacher-made assessment instruments. Finally, it should be restated at this point that the skills data that are collected from teacher-made and/or standardized tests should be verified or brought into question by observing and analyzing children as they attempt to use these skills in the act of reading.

■ ■ ■ **CHAPTER 9: PRACTICE**

1. Define what you believe diagnostic teaching to be.

_____

_____

_____

_____

_____

_____

_____

_____

2. To be effective, why is it necessary for teachers to become involved in diagnostic teaching?

_____

_____

_____

_____

_____

_____

_____

_____

3. List 3 out of the 5 general principles of diagnosis discussed in the chapter.

_____

_____

_____

_____

_____

_____

_____

_____

4. On a separate sheet of paper, construct an assessment instrument that measures beginning phonic skills. Include phonemic awareness (especially blending and segmentation activities), letter name knowledge, and initial consonant items.

5. On a separate sheet of paper, construct an assessment instrument that measures more advanced phonic skills. Include items that assess knowledge of consonant sounds in an ending position, consonant digraphs, consonant blends, long vowels, short vowels, vowel digraphs, special digraphs, and r-controlled vowels.

10

Phonics Post-Test

FILL IN THE BLANKS

1. _____ is a method in which basic phonetics, the study of human speech sounds, is used to teach beginning reading.
2. A(n) _____ is placed over a vowel letter to show that it is pronounced as a long sound.
3. A(n) _____ is two letters that stand for a single phoneme.
4. A(n) _____ syllable ends with a consonant phoneme.
5. Sounds in a syllable represented by two or more letters that do not lose their own identity when blended together are known as

   _____ _____ .

6. A(n) _____ is the smallest sound unit of a language that distinguishes one word from another.
7. A single vowel sound made of a blend of two vowel sounds in immediate sequence and pronounced in one syllable is known as a(n)

   _____ .

8. _____ , made up of a letter or combination of letters, represent phonemes.
9. A(n) _____ is a letter sequence comprised of a vowel grapheme and an ending consonant grapheme(s).
10. _____ are units of pronunciation consisting of a vowel alone or a vowel with one or more consonants.

TRUE–FALSE

_____ 11. The irregularity of consonant sounds is a basic problem of phonics.

_____ 12. The schwa sound usually has a consistent spelling.

_____ 13. Phonics is *not* the most important skill required for effective reading.

_____ 14. Almost any letter may, at some time, be silent.

_____ 15. A grapheme must be composed of one and only one letter.

_____ 16. Each syllable must contain only one vowel sound.

_____ 17. In attacking multisyllable words, children must syllabicate before applying vowel generalizations.

_____ 18. There are over 200 ways to spell the 44 phonemes.

_____ 19. By the time the average child enters school, his or her auditory discrimination skills are fully developed.

_____ 20. The history of phonics shows that a phonics approach to teaching reading has been looked upon favorably by most reading authorities over the past 50 years.

MULTIPLE CHOICE

_____ 21. Which of the following is a sound?
   a. consonant
   b. grapheme
   c. digraph
   d. none of the above

_____ 22. Which of the following words contains an open syllable?
   a. dove
   b. dog
   c. threw
   d. fire

_____ 23. Which of the following words contains a consonant digraph?
   a. blue
   b. string
   c. fly
   d. home

_____ 24. Which of the following words contains letters that represent a diphthong?
   a. show
   b. seat
   c. through
   d. out

_____ 25. How many phonemes are represented by the word *knight*?
   a. 2
   b. 3
   c. 4
   d. 5

_____ 26. How many phonemes are represented by the word *through*?
 a. 1
 b. 2
 c. 3
 d. 4

_____ 27. Which of the following pairs contains the same vowel phoneme?
 a. took–room
 b. grew–too
 c. food–wool
 d. none of the above

_____ 28. Which of the following letters do not represent phonemes that are identified by their own name?
 a. c and s
 b. b and d
 c. y and x
 d. x and c

_____ 29. Which of the following consonant letters are most phonemically inconsistent in representing more than one sound?
 a. b and d
 b. c and g
 c. r and t
 d. m and p

_____ 30. Which of the following letter pairs represents a consonant blend?
 a. th
 b. fl
 c. zh
 d. wh

_____ 31. Which of the following nonsense words would most likely represent the "soft c" sound?
 a. cumb
 b. cimp
 c. cople
 d. calobe

_____ 32. Which of the following nonsense words would most likely represent the "hard g" sound?
 a. gilture
 b. weg
 c. gymp
 d. tuge

_____ 33. Which of the following consonant letters affects the vowel
that precedes it?
   a. s
   b. t
   c. r
   d. none of the above

_____ 34. Which of the following words does *not* contain a consonant
blend?
   a. street
   b. chin
   c. brown
   d. fly

_____ 35. Which of the following words contains a closed syllable?
   a. grow
   b. why
   c. boy
   d. rote

Circle the item in each list that does not belong. Explain your reason
for each choice.

36. phoneme   digraph   diphthong   vowel

_____

_____

_____

37. th   tw   ch   ng   wh

_____

_____

_____

38. go   home   low   boy   high

_____

_____

_____

39. boy   pout   ounce   toil   double

_____

_____

_____

40. cuple   capon   cepp   cobat

_____

———————————————————————————————

———————————————————————————————

How many phonemes are represented in the following words? Write each word using its phoneme pronunciation symbols.

41. blue _____ _____

42. herd _____ _____

43. toxic _____ _____

44. should _____ _____

45. who _____ _____

46. air _____ _____

47. quit _____ _____

48. antique _____ _____

49. said _____ _____

50. school _____ _____

The following questions should be answered by using the vowel generalizations that are often taught in elementary schools. Each question will require the vowel pronunciation contained in a nonsense word.

_____ 51. The *i* in *dif* has the same sound as:
   a. girl
   b. in
   c. sight
   d. none of the above

_____ 52. The *u* in *smupe* has the same sound as:
   a. hurt
   b. pup
   c. use
   d. none of the above

_____ 53. The *a* in *kna* has the same sound as:
   a. mart
   b. ate
   c. map
   d. none of the above

_____ 54. The *e* in *reab* has the same sound as:
   a. bee
   b. err
   c. send
   d. none of the above

_____ 55. The *i* in *lirp* has the same sound as:
    a. bin
    b. high
    c. whirl
    d. none of the above

_____ 56. The *u* in *nupp* has the same sound as:
    a. hurt
    b. cup
    c. prude
    d. none of the above

_____ 57. The first *e* in *zeet* has the same sound as:
    a. me
    b. err
    c. send
    d. none of the above

_____ 58. The *u* in *tue* has the same sound as:
    a. cup
    b. hurt
    c. use
    d. none of the above

Indicate where the syllabic divisions occur in the following vowel–consonant patterns, nonsense words, or real words. Knowledge of syllabication generalizations is essential. There are no consonant digraphs in questions 49 through 52.

_____ 59. CVCVCC
    a. CV–CV–CC
    b. CVC–VCC
    c. CV–CVCC
    d. CVCV–CC

_____ 60. CVCCVC
    a. CV–CCVC
    b. CVCC–VC
    c. CVC–CVC
    d. CV–CC–VC

_____ 61. VCCVC
    a. VC–CVC
    b. V–CCVC
    c. VCC–VC
    d. VCCVC

_____ 62. CCVCVCC
    a. CCVC–VCC
    b. CCV–C–VCC
    c. CC–VC–VCC
    d. CCV–CVCC

_____ 63. ralagasins
    a. ra–la–ga–sins
    b. ral–a–ga–sins
    c. ral–ag–a–sins
    d. ra–la–gas–ins

_____ 64. soctaluca
    a. soc–ta–lu–ca
    b. soc–tal–u–ca
    c. soct–al–u–ca
    d. soct–a–lu–ca

_____ 65. plukle
    a. pluk–le
    b. plukle
    c. pl–u–kle
    d. plu–kle

_____ 66. exanphema
    a. exan–phe–ma
    b. ex–an–phe–ma
    c. ex–an–phem–a
    d. e–xan–phe–ma

_____ 67. megmer
    a. me–gmer
    b. meg–mer
    c. megm–er
    d. megmer

When children meet unknown words of more than one syllable, they must first be able to apply syllabication generalizations; second, they must be able to apply phonic generalizations. Using these generalizations, indicate how the following nonsense words would be pronounced correctly. (Although these words contain schwas, only long and short vowels will be used at this point.)

_____ 68. gebatt
    a. gēb–ătt
    b. gē–bătt
    c. gĕ–bătt
    d. gĕb–ātt

_____ 69. melkep
    a. mēl–kēp
    b. mē–lkĕp
    c. mĕl–kĕp
    d. mē–lkĕp

_____ 70. unstasal
    a. ŭn–stă–sāl
    b. ŭn–stăs–ăl
    c. ūns–tās–ăl
    d. ŭn–stā–săl

Answer Key

CHAPTER 1: PRACTICE

1. is not
2. second
3. contextual analysis, structural analysis
4. letters, sounds
5. synthetic
6. Answers will vary.
7. In learning phonics, children must have the opportunity to *see, hear,* and *say* the components they are being asked to learn. Initial instruction and practice in phonics should concentrate, therefore, on oral activities.
8. The purpose of phonics is to assist children in systematically decoding words that are unknown to them by teaching them the relationships that exist between letters and speech sounds. Phonics for phonics' sake should never be the goal of instruction.

CHAPTER 2: PHONICS PRETEST

1. b
2. f
3. h
4. e
5. a
6. d
7. j
8. i

9. c

10. g

11. true

12. false

13. false

14. true

15. true

16. false

17. true

18. false

19. false

20. false

21. b

22. c

23. b

24. d

25. c

26. c

27. b

28. d

29. b

30. b

31. a

32. b

33. c

34. b

35. b

36. *th* is a consonant digraph and the others are letters that represent consonant blends.

37. *st* represents a consonant blend, while the others are consonant digraphs.

38. *s* is the only letter that does not, at some time, represent a vowel sound.

39. *low* is the only word that does not contain letters representing the diphthong sound.

40. *gym* is the only word that contains a "soft g."

41. b

42. c

43. c

44. b

45. b

46. d

47. b

48. c

49. b

50. c

51. a

52. d

53. b

54. a

55. d

56. b

57. b

58. b

59. c

60. d

CHAPTER 2: PRACTICE

Answers will vary.

CUMULATIVE REVIEW OF CHAPTERS 1 AND 2

1. contextual analysis, structural analysis

2. is not

3. are

4. As children build larger sight vocabularies, they appear to rely less on phonics in many cases and more on the power of analogy: comparing unknown words to words that are known. Once children build this storehouse of words and progress beyond the beginning levels of reading, such elements as background knowledge, vocabulary, and general ability to reason become significantly more important in comprehending text.

5. *Explicit* or synthetic phonics emphasizes the learning of individual sounds, often in isolation, and follows with instruction that teaches chil-

dren how to blend these individual sounds to form words (a part-to-whole approach). *Implicit* or analytical phonics, on the other hand, begins with whole words and identifies individual sounds as parts of those words. Efforts are made to avoid pronouncing letter sounds in isolation (a whole-to-part approach).

6. Answers will vary.

7. Although the reader may pronounce an unknown word correctly, if it is not part of her speaking-listening vocabulary, she would have no way of knowing whether she was correct or not.

CHAPTER 3: PRACTICE

1. phoneme, vowel, rime, diphthong, consonant
2. a, e, i, o, u. y, w
3. go, dew, through
4. digraph
5. bri<u>ng</u>, <u>th</u>e, <u>sh</u>ut, <u>ch</u>ill
6. d<u>ew</u>, l<u>oo</u>k, s<u>ou</u>p, b<u>oy</u>, b<u>ea</u>t
7. diphthong, /ou/
8. sound
9. macron
10. breve
11. digraph
12. closed
13. digraph
14. phonetics
15. *Vowel:* sounds represented by *a, e, i, o, u,* and sometimes *y* and *w.*
    Grapheme: a letter or combination of letters that represents a phoneme.
    Phoneme: the smallest sound unit of a language that distinguishes one word from another.
    Consonant: sounds represented by any letter of the English alphabet except *a, e, i, o,* and *u.*
    Syllable: a unit of pronunciation that consists of a vowel alone or a vowel with one or more consonants. There is only one vowel phoneme in each syllable.
    Macron: the orthographic symbol, (-), placed over a vowel letter to show that it is pronounced as a long sound.
    Open syllable: any syllable that ends with a vowel phoneme.

Breve: the orthographic symbol, (ˇ), placed over a vowel letter to show that it is pronounced as a short sound.

Digraph: two letters that stand for a single phoneme.

Rime: the part of a syllable that includes the vowel sound and any consonant sound(s) following it.

CUMULATIVE REVIEW OF CHAPTERS 1 THROUGH 3

1. Phonics helps only if the unknown word is part of the reader's speaking-listening vocabulary.

2. whole-word. *Pneumonia* does not follow many phonic generalizations, especially vowel generalizations. Consequently, efforts spent with a whole-word emphasis would most likely produce better results.

3. do not believe. Answers will vary.

4. Synthetic, Analytic. Answers will vary.

5. Answers will vary.

6. Answers will vary.

7. A *digraph* is two *letters* that stand for a single phoneme, while a *diphthong* is a single vowel *sound* made up of a glide from one vowel to another. For example, in the word *oil*, the letters *oi* form the digraph while the sound /oi/ is the diphthong.

8. blend, street

9. Answers will vary.

10. A consonant digraph is two *letters* that stand for a single sound. A consonant blend is a combination of *sounds* in a syllable represented by two or more letters that are blended together without losing their own identity.

CHAPTER 4: PRACTICE

1. Answers will vary for this practice.

CUMULATIVE REVIEW OF CHAPTERS 1 THROUGH 4

1. rime

2. diphthong

3. rime

4. open

5. consonant blend

6. schwa

7. breve

8. diphthong

9. true, false

10. Answers will vary.

11. *Phoneme:* the smallest unit of a language that distinguishes one word from another.
    Grapheme: a letter or combination of letters that represents a phoneme.
    Digraph: two letters that stand for a single phoneme.
    Onset: the consonant sound(s) of a syllable that comes before the vowel sound.

12. Answers will vary.

CHAPTER 5: PRACTICE

1. 44, 25, 19

2. inconsistent

3. vowel sounds

4. too—shoes

5. a. coil   /oi/
   b. out   /ou/
   d. owl   /ou/

6. *c, q, x*

7. /s/   /zh/
   /k/   /f/
   /n/   /j/
   /sh/   /h/
   /ng/   /g/
   /hw/   /k/

8. /ā/   /û/
   /ī/   /ă/
   /oi/   /ou/
   /ū/   /ŏo/
   /ŏ/   /ĕ/
   /ōo/   /ŭ/

9. 3, /s/ /ī/ /t/
   2, /s/ /ō/
   3, /s/ /ĭ/ /ng/
   3, /b/ /l/ /ōo/
   4, /g/ /ō/ /s/ /t/

3, /sh/ /ĭ/ /p/
3, /ō/ /l/ /d/
2, /b/ /oi/
4, /b/ /û/ /r/ /d/
3, /b/ /ō/ /th/
4, /b/ /ŏ/ /k/ /s/
4, /s/ /ĕ/ /n/ /t/
3, /k/ /ō/ /m/
2, /k/ /ou/
2, /l/ /ō/

CUMULATIVE REVIEW OF CHAPTERS 1 THROUGH 5

1. a. Different children will find some methods more suited to their abilities than others. Thus, each child should be given opportunities to learn and use all word-recognition methods.
   b. Some words are learned more easily by one method than by another.
2. Phonics
3. consonant phoneme (sound)
4. grapheme
5. false
6. syllable
7. schwa
8. near-point
9. Auditory acuity
10. false. The relationship is not one of cause and effect. Knowledge of letter names does not cause one to become a better reader.
11. Visual discrimination must be done with letters and/or words. Practice with geometric figures and pictures does not transfer to the type of visual discrimination needed for reading.
12. Answers will vary.
13. *Mental Measurement Yearbooks*
14. 4, /p/ /l/ /ŭ/ /m/
    2, /ô/ /f/
    5, /f/ /ū/ /ch/ /û/ /r/
    5, /n/ /ā/ /k/ /ĭ/ /d/
    3, /t/ /r/ /o͞o/
    4, /p/ /l/ /ū/ /m/
    4, /f/ /ŭ/ /n/ /ē/

4, /k/ /w/ /ē/ /n/
4, /m/ /ĭ/ /k/ /s/
3, /h/ /â/ /r/

CHAPTER 6: PRACTICE

1. consonant, vowel
2. cint, cymp, sluce
3. /ch/, /k/, /sh/
4. only one, is
5. Inductive
6. gultion, seg
7. silent
8. consonant digraph, /k/
9. c
10. a
11. c
12. a
13. b
14. d
15. c
16. b
17. . . . it is not the final letter.
18. . . . it is the final letter.
19. long, silent
20. long, silent

CUMULATIVE REVIEW OF CHAPTERS 1 THROUGH 6

1. false
2. phonetics
3. macron
4. vowel
5. smallest
6. digraph
7. Auditory discrimination

8. is not. It is quite possible that a child will be ready to learn under one set of instructional conditions and not be ready to learn under another.

9. /ă/   /ô/
   /ŭ/   /ə/
   /o͝o/   /ĕ/
   /ĭ/   /û/

10. /j/   /hw/
    /g/   /f/
    /k/   /k/ /s/
    /h/   /s/

11. 3, /f/ /ō/ /n/
    2, /ou/ /t/
    2, /n/ /o͞o/
    4, /ə/ /b/ /ou/ /t/
    3, /ô/ /t/ /ō/
    3, /k/ /o͝o/ /d/
    2, /t/ /oi/
    4, /p/ /û/ /r/ /l/
    5, /p/ /o͝o/ /d/ /ĭ/ /ng/
    3, /d/ /â/ /r/

CHAPTER 7: PRACTICE

1. vowel sounds

2. 19

3. is not

4. c   /s/, /k/ (Answers for words will vary.)
   g   /g/, /j/
   s   /s/, /z/
   x   /z/
            /k/ /s/
            /g/ /z/

5. /s/
   /k/
   /j/
   /g/

6. consonant blends

7. B   B   D   B
   D   D   B   B

B	D	B	D
D	B	D	B
D	B	B	B

8. Vowel sounds are far more stable within particular phonograms than they are in isolation.

9. Answers will vary.

10. Answers will vary.

11. Answers will vary.

CUMULATIVE REVIEW OF CHAPTERS 1 THROUGH 7

1. does not appear

2. second

3. *Phonics:* A method in which basic phonetics is used to teach reading.
   Phoneme: The smallest sound unit of a language that distinguishes one word from another.
   Open syllable: Any syllable that ends with a vowel phoneme.
   Macron: The symbol (-) placed over a vowel letter to show it is pronounced as a long sound.
   Consonant: A sound represented by any letter of the English alphabet except *a, e, i, o, u.*
   Digraph: Two letters that stand for a single phoneme (sound).
   Syllable: A unit of pronunciation consisting of a vowel alone or a vowel with one or more consonants. There is only one vowel phoneme in each syllable.

4. reading, writing

5. out, book, that
   song, chat, knob

6. grapheme

7. "Emergent literacy is concerned with the earliest phases of literacy development, the period between birth and the time when children read and write conventionally. The term *emergent literacy* signals a belief that, in a literate society, young children—even 1- and 2-year olds—are in the process of becoming literate" (Sulzby & Teale, 1991, p. 728). Thus, if young children have had little opportunity to experiment with reading and writing before they enter school, it can have a significant negative impact on their achievement.

8. The *Yearbooks* provide evaluative information regarding the strengths and weaknesses of a variety of standardized tests.

9. Answers will vary. However, the fact that the relationship is not one of cause and effect should be included in the answer. Knowledge of letter names does not cause one to become a better reader.

10. /k/   /k/ /w/
    /h/   /k/ /s/
    silent   /s/
    /zh/   /k/

11. /â/   /ō/
    /ə/   /ô/
    /ŏ/   /ou/
    /û/   /o͝o/

12. 3, /r/ /ĕ/ /d/
    3, /k/ /ō/ /t/
    3, /hw/ /ē/ /l/
    4, /k/ /w/ /ĭ/ /t/
    2, /h/ /o͞o/
    3, /hw/ /ĕ/ /n/
    3, /f/ /l/ /ī/
    4, /k/ /û/ /r/ /s/
    7, /d/ /ĭ/ /ə/ /l/ /ĕ/ /k/ /t/

13. *Coat:* When two successive vowel letters occur in a syllable and they are not any of the special digraphs (oi, oy, ow, ou, oo, au), the first is usually long and the second is silent (especially ee—keep, ea—meat, ai—pain, ay—say, oa—load).
    Hope: When two vowel letters in a syllable are separated by a consonant and one is a final *e,* the first usually records its long sound and the *e* is silent.
    She: A single vowel letter in a syllable usually represents the long sound if it is the final letter.
    But: A single vowel letter in a syllable usually represents the short sound if it is not the final letter.

14. The term *generalizations* better represents the fact that there are exceptions to the letter–sound associations we teach children.

CHAPTER 8: PRACTICE

1. first
2. vowel

3. are

4. d, t

5. Although double consonant letters are generally separated when words are broken into syllables via writing, the sound will be represented in only one syllable.

6. are not

7. one

8. *Vowel-Consonant Letter Patterns*

    a. V-CVC   #9

    b. CVC-CV   #8

    c. CCVC-CVC   #8

    d. CCV-CVC   #9

Real Words

    e. a-mass   #9

    f. a-phis   #6, #9

    g. bel-dam   #8

    h. bo-lide   #9

    i. cu-pule   #9

    j. dis-pen-sar-y   #2, #8

    k. fur-be-low   #5, #8, #9

    l. ju-di-ca-ture #2, #9

Nonsense Words

    m. pre-an-the-ma   #2, #6, #8, #9

    n. un-bot-ed   #2, #2b

    o. e-ma-kle   #4, #9

    p. e-pe-ture   #2a, #9

    q. gra-peet   #5, #9

    r. re-sired   #2, #2b

    s. e-cad   #9

    t. an-tole   #8

    u. scrnt   no vowel letter, no vowel sound, no word

    v. ma-shot   #6, #9

    w. haulm   #5

    x. sub-ton-en   #2

    y. lat-ton   #7, #8

CUMULATIVE REVIEW OF CHAPTERS 1 THROUGH 8

1. No. To be effective, phonics instruction must be oral in nature. Children need to hear and speak the language to get the full benefit of instruction.

2. *Phonetics:* The scientific study of human speech sounds.
   Grapheme: A letter or combination of letters that represents a phoneme.
   Vowels: Sounds represented by *a, e, i, o, u,* and sometimes *y* and *w.*
   Diphthong: A single vowel sound made up of a glide from one vowel to another in immediate sequence and pronounced in one syllable.
   Consonant blend: Sounds in a syllable represented by two or more letters that are blended together without losing their own identity.
   Rime: The part of a syllable that includes the vowel sound and any consonant sound(s) that come after it.
   Schwa: An unstressed sound commonly occurring in unstressed syllables. It closely resembles the sound of a short *u.*

3. Reading is a visual act that requires effective near-point vision. Yet the types of tests often administered to children at the beginning stages of school measure only far-point vision.

4. Research has shown that a positive relationship exists between oral language and reading achievement. Oral language appears to serve as an essential foundation on which reading instruction can and should be built.

5. Segmentation is the process of isolating all the sounds of a word, while blending is the process of recognizing isolated speech sounds and the ability to pronounce the word for which they stand. Examples will vary.

6. /ă/   /zh/
   /â/   /ng/
   /ī/   /k/
   /oi/   /g/

7. Teachers should verify that the phonic generalizations they are being asked to teach have enough utility to justify teaching them.

8. The inductive process begins with specifics and moves to generalizations about them, while the deductive process begins with generalizations that are then applied to specific words. No. It would appear that both approaches have their place in phonics instruction.

9. consonant. Consonants are more consistent in their spelling than are vowel sounds. Written English has a left-to-right orientation whereby the initial position of words assumes the most significant position in word recognition. Most of the words that children are initially asked to learn begin with consonant sounds.

10. Answers will vary.

11. As children begin to work with an increasing number of unknown polysyllabic words, they must be able to syllabicate them correctly first before applying vowel generalizations.

CHAPTER 9: PRACTICE

1. Diagnostic teaching is the process whereby teachers identify students' strengths and weaknesses through both formal and informal means, and use this diagnostic information to direct their instructional actions.

2. Unless teachers have diagnostic information to assist in the identification of the strengths and weaknesses of students, it is extremely difficult to set up instructional programs that allow students the opportunity to grow to their full potential.

3. a. Diagnosis should be viewed as a daily occurrence.
   b. Decisions about children should be based on diagnostic information collected from a variety of sources.
   c. The identification of *patterns of error* should be emphasized when analyzing diagnostic information.
   d. Work on only one or two reading weaknesses at a time.
   e. Diagnosis for its own sake is not acceptable; it must lead to specific instructional action.

4. Answers will vary.

5. Answers will vary.

CHAPTER 10: PHONICS POST-TEST

1. Phonics
2. macron
3. digraph
4. closed
5. consonant blends
6. phoneme
7. diphthong
8. Graphemes
9. phonogram
10. Syllables
11. false
12. false

13. true
14. true
15. false
16. true
17. true
18. true
19. false
20. false
21. a
22. c
23. b
24. d
25. b
26. c
27. b
28. d
29. b
30. b
31. b
32. b
33. c
34. b
35. d
36. *digraph* refers to letters whereas the other terms refer to sounds.
37. *tw* represents a consonant blend, while the others are consonant digraphs.
38. *boy* is the only word that contains letters that represent the diphthong sound.
39. *double* is the only word that does not contain letters representing the diphthong sound.
40. *cepp* is the only word that contains a "soft c."
41. 3, /b/ /l/ /o͞o/
42. 4, /h/ /û/ /r/ /d/
43. 6, /t/ /ŏ/ /k/ /s/ /ĭ/ /k/
44. 3, /sh/ /o͝o/ /d/
45. 2, /h/ /o͞o/

46. 2, /â/ /r/
47. 4, /k/ /w/ /ĭ/ /t/
48. 5, /ă/ /n/ /t/ /ē/ /k/
49. 3, /s/ /ĕ/ /d/
50. 4, /s/ /k/ /o͞o/ /l/
51. b
52. c
53. b
54. a
55. c
56. b
57. a
58. c
59. c
60. c
61. a
62. d
63. a
64. a
65. d
66. b
67. b
68. b
69. c
70. d

Glossary

accent (primary): The syllable in a word that receives the strongest and loudest emphasis.

analytic phonics: A whole-to-part phonics approach that emphasizes starting with whole words and identifying individual sounds as part of those words. Efforts are generally made to avoid pronouncing letter sounds in isolation. Also known as implicit phonics.

auditory discrimination: The ability to hear similarities and differences between sounds as they occur in spoken words.

base word: A word to which prefixes and/or suffixes are added to create new but related words. The simplest member of a word family.

breve: An orthographic symbol, (ˇ), placed above vowel graphemes to indicate pronunciation.

circumflex: An orthographic symbol, (ˆ), placed above vowel graphemes to indicate pronunciation.

closed syllable: Any syllable ending with a consonant phoneme. Examples: come /m/; love /v/; ran /n/.

compound word: A word made up of two or more base words.

consonants: Sounds represented by any letter of the English alphabet except *a, e, i, o,* and *u.* Consonants are *sounds* that are made by closing or restricting the breath channel.

consonant blend: Sounds in a syllable represented by two or more letters that are blended together without losing their own identity. Examples: blue /b/ /l/; brown /b/ /r/; twig /t/ /w/; street /s/ /t/ /r/; flip /f/ /l/.

decoding: The process of determining the pronunciation of an unknown word.

deductive instruction: Instructional procedure that centers on telling children about generalizations and having them apply the generalizations to specific words; a general-to-specific emphasis.

digraph: Two letters that stand for a single phoneme. Examples: thin /th/; each /ē/; shop /sh/; boy /oi/; look /o͝o/; rang /ng/; few /o͞o/. A digraph is simply a grapheme of two letters.

116

diphthong: A single vowel sound made up of a blend of two vowel sounds in immediate sequence and pronounced in one syllable. Examples: /oi/ in *oil* and *boy*; /ou/ in *house* and *owl*. (Phonetics would consider that some single-letter vowels are actually diphthongs. For the purposes of teaching reading, however, only /oi/ and /ou/ will be considered diphthongs.)

grapheme: A letter or combination of letters that represents a phoneme. Examples: the phoneme /b/ in *bat* is represented by the grapheme *b*; the phoneme /f/ in *phone* is represented by the grapheme *ph*. There are over 200 different ways to spell the phonemes. For example, /f/ can take the form of *f* in *fine, gh* in *cough,* and *ph* in *elephant.* This is an example of three different graphemes representing the same phoneme.

inductive instruction: Instructional procedure that begins with an analysis of specifics from which generalizations are formed; a specific-to-general emphasis.

macron: An orthographic symbol, (-), placed over a vowel letter to show that it is pronounced as a long sound (sometimes called glided vowels).

onset: The consonant sound(s) of a syllable that come before the vowel sound. (See the definition of *rime* for examples of *onsets.*)

open syllable: Any syllable ending with a vowel phoneme. Examples: see /ē/; may /ā/; boy /oi/; auto /ō/.

phoneme: The smallest *sound* unit of a language that distinguishes one word from another. Examples: the phoneme /h/ distinguishes *hat* from *at*; the words *tell* and *yell* are distinguished by their initial phonemes /t/ and /y/, respectively.

phoneme blending: The process of recognizing isolated speech sounds and the ability to pronounce the word for which they stand.

phoneme segmentation: The ability of isolating all the sounds of a word.

phonemic awareness: The ability to recognize spoken words as a sequence of individual sounds.

phonetics: The scientific study of human speech sounds.

phonics: A method in which basic phonetics, the study of human speech sounds, is used to teach beginning reading.

phonogram: A letter sequence comprised of a vowel grapheme and an ending consonant grapheme(s), such as *-ig* in *wig, dig,* and *big,* or *-ack* in *back, tack,* and *sack.*

r-controlled vowel: When a vowel letter is followed by the letter *r*, it makes the vowel sound neither long nor short. For example, in *her,* the vowel sound becomes /û/; in *dare*, it becomes /â/.

rime: The part of a syllable that includes the vowel sound and any consonant sound(s) that come after it. The graphic representation of a rime is referred to as a *phonogram.* For example, in the word *mat,* the onset is /m/ and the rime is /at/.

root: Often used as a synonym for *base word.*

schwa sound: An unstressed sound commonly occurring in unstressed syllables. It is represented by the symbol, /ə/, and closely resembles the short sound for *u*. Examples: *a* in *about*; *o* in *occur*; *i* in *pencil*; *u* in *circus*.

syllable: A unit of pronunciation consisting of a vowel alone or a vowel with one or more consonants. There can be only one vowel phoneme (sound) in each syllable.

synthetic phonics: A part-to-whole phonics approach that emphasizes the learning of individual sounds, often in isolation, and combining them to form words. Also known as explicit phonics.

umlaut: An orthographic symbol, (¨), placed above vowel graphemes to indicate pronunciation.

visual discrimination: The ability to visually perceive similarities and differences (in reading, this means to perceive similarities and differences between written letters and words).

vowels: Sounds represented by *a, e, i, o, u,* and sometimes *y* and *w,* in the English alphabet. Vowels are sounds that are made without closing or restricting the breath channel.

References

Adams, M. J. (1990). *Beginning to read: Thinking and learning about print.* Cambridge, MA: The MIT Press.

Anderson, R. C., Hiebert, E. H., Scott, J. A., & Wilkinson, I. A. G. (1984). *Becoming a nation of readers: The report of the commission on reading.* Washington, DC: National Institute of Education, U.S. Department of Education.

Ausubel, D. P. (1959, February). Viewpoints from related disciplines: Human growth and development. *Teachers College Record, 60,* 245–254.

Bailey, M. H. (1967, February). The utility of phonic generalizations in grades one through six. *The Reading Teacher, 20,* 413–418.

Blackman, B. A. (1984, August). Relationship of rapid naming ability and language analysis skills to kindergarten and first-grade reading achievement. *Journal of Educational Psychology, 76,* 610–622.

Bond, G. L., & Dykstra, R. (1967). *Final report, project no. X-001.* Washington, DC: Bureau of Research, Office of Education, U.S. Department of Health, Education, and Welfare.

Bond, G. L., Tinker, M. A., Wasson, B. B., & Wasson, J. B. (1989). *Reading difficulties: Their diagnosis and correction* (6th ed.). Englewood Cliffs, NJ: Prentice Hall.

Bradley, L., & Bryant, P. E. (1983, February). Categorizing sounds and learning to read—A causal connection. *Nature, 301,* 419–421.

Burmeister, L. E. (1966). *An evaluation of the inductive and deductive group approaches to teaching selected word analysis generalizations to disabled readers in eighth and ninth grade.* Unpublished doctoral dissertation, University of Wisconsin.

Burmeister, L. E. (1968, February). Vowel pairs. *The Reading Teacher, 21,* 445–452.

Caldwell, E. C., Roth, S. R., & Turner, R. R. (1978, Spring). A reconsideration of phonic generalizations. *Journal of Reading Behavior, 10,* 91–96.

Calfee, R. C., Lindamood, P., & Lindamood, C. (1973, June). Acoustic-phonetic skills and reading—Kindergarten through twelfth grade. *Journal of Educational Psychology, 64,* 293–298.

Chall, J. (1967). *Learning to read: The great debate.* New York: McGraw-Hill.

Chall, J. (1983). *Learning to read: The great debate* (2nd ed.). New York: McGraw-Hill.

Clymer, T. (1963, January). The utility of phonic generalizations in the primary grades. *The Reading Teacher, 16,* 252–258.

Conoley, J. C., & Impara, J. C. (Eds.). (1995). *Twelfth mental measurement yearbook.* The Buros Institute of Mental Measurements. Lincoln, NE: University of Nebraska—Lincoln.

Durkin, D. (1993). *Teaching them to read* (6th ed.). Boston: Allyn & Bacon.

Edmiaston, R. K. (1984, July/August). Oral language and reading: How are they related for third graders? *Remedial and Special Education, 5,* 33–37.

Ehri, L. C. (1979). Linguistic insight: Threshold of reading acquisition. In T. G. Waller & G. E. MacKinnon (Eds.), *Reading research: Advances in theory and practice* (Vol. 1, 63–114). New York: Academic Press.

Ekwall, E. (1976). *Diagnosis and remediation of the disabled reader.* Boston: Allyn & Bacon.

Ekwall, E. (1986). *Ekwall reading inventory* (2nd ed.). Newton, MA: Allyn and Bacon.

Emans, R. (1967, February). The usefulness of phonic generalizations above the primary grades. *The Reading Teacher, 20,* 419–425.

Emans, R. (1968, May). History of phonics. *Elementary English, 45,* 602–608.

Flavell, J. (1977). *Cognitive development.* Englewood Cliffs, NJ: Prentice Hall.

Flesch, R. (1955). *Why Johnny can't read.* New York: Harper Press.

Fuld, P. (1968, February). Vowel sounds in VCC words. *The Reading Teacher, 21,* 442–444.

Gates, L. (1986, Summer). The consonant generalizations revisited. *Reading Horizons, 26,* 232–236.

Golinkoff, R. M. (1978). Critique: Phonemic awareness skills and reading achievement. In F. B. Murray & L. L. Pikulski (Eds.), *The acquisition of reading: Cognitive linguistic, and perceptual prerequisites* (23–41). Baltimore, MD: University Park Press.

Groff, P. J. (1984, January). Resolving the letter name controversy. *The Reading Teacher, 37,* 384–388.

Harris, L. A., & Smith, C. B. (1986). *Reading instruction: Diagnostic teaching in the classroom* (4th ed.). New York: Macmillan.

Heilman, A. W. (1981). *Phonics in proper perspective* (4th ed.). Columbus, OH: Merrill.

Hillerich, R. L. (1978, April). Reading: Phonics—What about the rules? *Teacher, 95* (8), 94.

Houghton Mifflin. (1997a). *Family treasurers,* Level 1.5 teacher's edition. Boston, MA.

Houghton Mifflin (1997b). *Try it my way,* Level 5 teacher's edition. Boston, MA.

Houghton Mifflin (1997c). *Unexpected guests,* Level 1.4 teacher's edition. Boston, MA.

Johns, J. L. (1991). *Basic reading inventory* (5th ed.). Dubuque, IA: Kendall/Hunt.

Lewkowicz, N. K. (1980, October). Phonemic awareness training: What to teach and how to teach it. *Journal of Educational Psychology, 72,* 686–700.

Nation, A., & Hulme, C. (1997, April–June). Phonemic segmentation, not onset-rime segmentation, predicts early reading and spelling skills. *Reading Research Quarterly, 32,* 154–167.

Pflaum, S. W., Walberg, H. J., Karegianes, M. L., & Rasher, S. P. (1980, July/August). Reading instruction: A quantitative analysis. *Educational Researcher, 9,* 12–18.

Rosenthal, A. S., Baker, K., & Ginsburg, A. (1983, October). The effects of language background on achievement level and learning among elementary school students. *Sociology of Education, 56,* 157–169.

Searfoss, L. W., & Readence, J. E. (1994). *Helping children learn to read* (3rd ed.). Boston: Allyn and Bacon.

Silvaroli, N. J. (1994). *Classroom reading inventory* (7th ed.). Dubuque, IA: Brown & Benchmark.

Silver Burdett Ginn. (1993). *Make a wish.* Level 1.5 teacher's edition. Needham, MA.

Smith, F. (1982). *Understanding reading* (3rd ed.). New York: Holt, Rinehart & Winston.

Spache, G. D., Andres, M. C., Curtis, H. A., Rowland, M. L., & Fields, M. H. (1965). *A longitudinal first-grade reading readiness program* (Cooperative Research Project No. 2742). Tallahassee, FL: Florida State Department of Education.

Spache, G. D., & Spache, E. B. (1986). *Reading in the elementary school* (5th ed.). Boston: Allyn & Bacon.

Stahl, S. A., Osborn, J., & Lehr, F. (1990). *Beginning to read: thinking and learning about print—A summary.* University of Illinois at Urbana—Champaign: Center for the Study of Reading, The Reading Research and Education Center.

Sulzby, E., & Teale, W. (1991). Emergent literacy. In R. Barr, M. L. Kamil, P. B. Mosenthal, & P. D. Pearson (Eds.), *Handbook of reading research: Volume II* (pp. 727–757). New York: Longman.

Thorndike, E. L., & Lorge, I. (1944). *The teacher's book of 30,000 words.* New York: Bureau of Publications, Teachers College, Columbia University.

Trelease, J. (1995). *The new read-aloud handbook* (3rd ed.). New York: Viking Penguin.

Tunmer, W. E., & Nesdale, A. R. (1985, August). Phonemic segmentation skill and beginning reading. *Journal of Educational Psychology, 77,* 417–427.

Wylie, R. R., & Durrell, D. D. (1970). Teaching vowels through phonograms. *Elementary English, 47,* 787–791.